# BANKING ON OPPORTUNITY

## A SCAN OF THE EVOLVING FIELD OF BANK ON INITIATIVES

 **US DEPARTMENT OF THE TREASURY**

Office of Financial Education and Financial Access

Prepared by the National League of Cities Institute for Youth, Education and Families under contract with CFED and the U.S. Department of the Treasury. Assistance was additionally provided by CFED, the New America Foundation, and the San Francisco Office of Financial Empowerment.

Contract Number: GS-10F-0177L
Order Number: TDOX11-F-0036

2011

# Table of Contents

# EXECUTIVE SUMMARY

Since its successful inception in 2006 in the city of San Francisco, the Bank On model has gained support from state and local officials across the U.S. as a way of bringing unbanked and underbanked consumers into the financial mainstream. In addition to connecting unbanked individuals to low-cost accounts, Bank On initiatives involve efforts to raise public awareness, provide targeted outreach, and expand access to financial education. The appeal of Bank On is straightforward: it addresses the widely-recognized challenge of financial access through interventions that are low-cost and responsive to the needs of both consumers and providers of basic financial services. There are currently dozens of communities that have implemented Bank On initiatives, and many more are planned.

## Current Situation and Findings

In general, Bank On programs benefit from strong leadership provided by local or state government leaders. Local governments have been engaged in most Bank On programs developed to date and play a lead coordinating role in most programs. However, it should be noted that while local authorities play a pivotal role in bringing together the initiative, the effectiveness of the Bank On model is actually driven primarily by the partnerships formed among local governments, financial institutions, community groups and nonprofit organizations, and financial regulators. Each Bank On partner plays a unique role in program development and implementation. Because of the nature of the model, no one entity could successfully create and manage a Bank On initiative without the others.

A key foundational component of Bank On programs is the transaction account that is offered to unbanked consumers. Thus, Bank On program leaders carefully negotiate the product criteria with financial institutions to ensure that they meet the needs of the target population. At the same time, participating financial institutions need to feel comfortable with a product that will meet their business needs. A compromise is usually necessary among the parties to ensure that everyone's objectives are met. Some of the most common baseline products offered by financial institutions to the unbanked as part of the Bank On initiative include no or low monthly account fees and minimum monthly balance, flexibility in opening accounts for individuals who have a record in ChexSystems, ways to minimize overdraft fees, and acceptance of alternative forms of identification such as the Mexican consular card. Many financial institutions participating in Bank On initiatives have also offered other products that meet the specific needs of the unbanked and underbanked populations in their communities.

Furthermore, in today's ever evolving financial marketplace, individuals who possess limited knowledge on how to navigate the financial system are at a disadvantage. Accordingly, all Bank On initiatives to date have included some type of financial education component. Having accessible financial education available to prospective Bank On customers not only gives them opportunities to learn how to best use financial products and services, but also alleviates financial institutions' hesitation to reach out to these traditionally high-risk individuals. Bank On initiatives typically offer financial education through existing providers, and often develop a set of financial education standards that providers should meet, covering important basic financial concepts.

Other critical components of Bank On initiatives include their marketing and outreach strategies. Most communities designate a specific committee of Bank On partners to coordinate marketing and outreach; some turn to communications firms to help coordinate their advertising campaigns. Additionally, 28 Bank On initiatives have signed a Memorandum of Understanding (MOU) with the City and County of San Francisco that allows them to use the City's own marketing materials to promote their respective Bank On programs, thereby lowering costs. Popular media used to promote Bank Ons include radio, newspapers, billboards, bus ads, and websites.

These aspects, among others, are critical to the successful implementation of a Bank On initiative. When combined with comprehensive preliminary research on community needs, early involvement of local elected officials and financial institutions, organized planning structures and the setting of measurable goals, Bank On initiatives can become highly successful and effective in carrying out their expectations.

## Challenges Facing Bank On Initiatives

While the Bank On model is a promising new approach for expanding access to safe, affordable financial services for unbanked individuals, many programs have invariably faced challenges. One of the most pervasive problems facing Bank On initiatives has been tracking the appropriate data, and using it to assess the impact and efficacy of the programs. Tracking and evaluation have proved difficult because financial institutions are often limited in the information that they are able or willing to collect, and local governments and other partners do not have regulatory authority to enforce data collection. It is generally infeasible for financial institutions to track consumer outcomes beyond the aggregate number of accounts opened and basic account activity; they generally do not collect information about customers such as gender, ethnicity, and other demographic data for account opening. Due to this lack of individual-level data, it is difficult to fully gauge how Bank On programs affect the communities they serve, influence the financial behaviors of customers who open accounts with them, and determine the reasons behind customers who end up closing their accounts.

Additional challenges Bank On initiatives are currently facing include maintaining momentum and further expanding the initiatives in order to enable them to reach out to more individuals. Newly implemented Bank On programs are hesitant to stray from the products that older programs are offering; this has inadvertently led the product criteria originally developed by Bank On San Francisco to become the "ceiling" to many Bank On programs. In fact, many subsequent initiatives have struggled with great efforts to convince financial institutions to offer additional beneficial features outside of the original Bank On San Francisco product such as the elimination overdraft protection charges, providing free money orders, capping monthly fees, or removing opening balance requirements. Furthermore, the changing regulatory environment of financial institutions may also serve as an impediment to Bank On programs. Recent research suggests financial institutions are becoming less willing to offer products to higher-risk markets or lower income consumers. These changes can impact Bank On initiatives as financial institutions reconsider the type of products to offer to the unbanked population.

## Future Directions

A Bank On initiative is flexible and easy to build upon in the sense that it can offer a platform for testing and delivering other innovative financial products for underserved populations. Limited evidence about account openings at this point suggest that Bank On programs appear to open new pathways for financial access for those individuals that were previously unbanked. Since access to mainstream financial services is only one step (albeit a very important one) towards financial security, future strategies to expand upon Bank On programs involve tying them together with other asset-building strategies. For instance, having Bank On programs work with initiatives like America Saves or AutoSave would continue to promote to Bank On customers the importance of savings and accumulating assets, ultimately making them more financial stable in the long run.

The Bank On field is still relatively young, but there is great potential to build upon and continue the successes that have been observed at both a local and state level, and ultimately create a nationwide initiative that attends to the needs of underserved families, and works to eradicate financial instability throughout the country.

Banking on Opportunity
A Scan of the Evolving Field of Bank On Initiatives          US DEPARTMENT OF THE TREASURY          5
Office of Financial Education and Financial Access

# Introduction

Since the first Bank On program was launched in San Francisco in 2006, this model of financial access has been refined, replicated, and identified as a leading strategy for state and local officials across the U.S. to bring unbanked and underbanked consumers into the financial mainstream. The Bank On concept is defined throughout this document as an initiative in which low-cost transaction and savings accounts are made available to unbanked individuals by federally insured banks and credit unions, on terms that are generally appropriate to people who have not had experience with such accounts, or have had previous poor experiences, and in which trusted community partners, such as government agencies and non-profit organizations encourage account opening and provide access to financial education. These programs are voluntary for all participants, and while there are many similarities across initiatives, key factors vary based on local needs. Bank On initiatives thrive upon collaborative partnerships among local government, financial institutions and community-based non-profit organizations. In addition to connecting unbanked individuals to low-cost bank accounts, Bank On programs involve efforts to raise public awareness, provide targeted outreach, and expand access to financial education. The appeal of Bank On is straightforward: it addresses the widely-recognized challenge of financial access through interventions that are low-cost and responsive to the needs of both consumers and providers of basic financial services.

Research has thoroughly documented the size of the unbanked[1] and underbanked[2] population nationwide and the risks and costs associated with over-reliance on alternative financial services. These challenges are of particular interest to policymakers who view efforts to increase underserved consumers' access to and use of basic banking services as an economic mobility strategy. Elected officials from different political parties and ideological backgrounds have championed Bank On initiatives because they offer an important service to residents without requiring new regulations or other legal mandates. Rather, Bank On relies on flexible, voluntary partnerships to achieve results. Private sector partners in a Bank On program gain access to new customers (many of whom have the capacity to transition into more frequently used and profitable products and services) and community goodwill. Consumers benefit from access to a safe place to keep their money, savings generated by using less-expensive services, more affordable credit products, and improved financial knowledge and capability. Additionally, the establishment of emergency savings to weather financial distress is beneficial to consumers. Communities benefit from more economically stable residents and can have additional positive outcomes from building collaboratives among financial institutions, non-profit organizations, government agencies and other entities.

The flexibility inherent in the Bank On model also allows it to be tailored to meet the needs of a diverse range of communities. Cities, counties, regions and states have all successfully adapted Bank On to their unique requirements. Urban, suburban and rural areas alike have launched Bank On initiatives that are appropriate for different community needs and opportunities.

---

1  Unbanked is defined throughout this report as those who do not have either a checking or savings account.  This definition is based on the FDIC National Survey of Unbanked and Underbanked Households, December 2009. Available at: http://www.fdic.gov/householdsurvey/.  Hereafter cited as FDIC 2009.

2  Underbanked is defined throughout this report as those who have a checking or savings account, but rely on alternative financial services – specifically non-bank money orders and check-cashing services, payday loans, rent-to-own agreements, pawn shops or refund anticipation loans.  This definition is based on the FDIC National Survey of Unbanked and Underbanked Households, December 2009.

## About this Report

This report was prepared to provide background on the "Bank On" model, a new approach for expanding access to safe, affordable financial services for unbanked households. Although this field has grown and attracted significant attention in a short period of time, there has not yet been a comprehensive review of programs, or even a formal scan of how many programs exist and their locations.

The purpose of this report is to describe the landscape of Bank On programs, their origins, and their context within a broader financial access field. The report provides basic information about Bank On programs that currently exist, including information about program structure, partnerships, and funding as well as an assessment of successes, challenges, special considerations and gaps in the field. Rather than providing a comprehensive review of all Bank On programs, the report is designed to present existing knowledge about the field using a snapshot of information gathered at a specific point in time.

Information for this report comes from several sources:

- A Bank On program survey: The National League of Cities Institute for Youth, Education and Families (NLC) conducted an online survey of Bank On programs in October 2010. The survey was sent to nearly 100 known Bank On programs, including municipal and state initiatives that had already launched and those that were preparing to launch. Leaders of 49 programs responded to the survey.

- Research and information gathered for NLC's publication, *Bank On Cities: Connecting Residents to the Financial Mainstream*.[3]

- Research and analysis from CFED's forthcoming publication on the role of financial institutions in Bank On programs.

- Conversations with Bank On program staff: NLC conducted short interviews with staff from nine Bank On programs to obtain more detailed information about certain aspects of their programs that were not included in the survey.

- Research from experts in the field: NLC reviewed data and analysis developed by experts in the financial access field, including the Center for Financial Services Innovation (CFSI), the New America Foundation, the Brookings Institution, the U.S. Department of the Treasury, and others.

The rest of the report is organized into several sections that describe the overall financial access field, the emergence and growth of Bank On initiatives, details about the structure of existing programs, direct and indirect benefits and outcomes, key components of successful programs, challenges facing the Bank On field, and opportunities for expanding the reach and effectiveness of Bank On within the context of comprehensive financial access initiatives.

---

3 Available at: http://www.nlc.org/find-city-solutions/iyef/family-economic-success/asset-building/bank-on-cities-toolkit.

## Access to Banking: A Strategy for Building Financial Security

Research conducted by the Federal Deposit Insurance Corporation (FDIC) in 2009 found that more than a quarter of U.S. households rely on alternative financial services to manage their money. Of these 30 million households, nine million are "unbanked" – they do not have a checking or a savings account. Twenty-one million are "underbanked" – they may have a checking or savings account but still use costly alternative financial services.[4]

### Why Does Access to Banking Matter?

A checking account with a bank or credit union, or a fully functional reloadable pre-paid card, provides a family with the means to make the basic financial transactions necessary for day-to-day life and facilitates saving. Individuals without a safe place to store their money are at greater risk of being victims of theft, have no way to access money remotely in the event of a disaster and are less likely to build assets.[5] Without access to mainstream financial services, individuals may spend tens of thousands of dollars over a lifetime on the high fees associated with check cashing, money orders, and other alternative financial services. According to a study by the Brookings Institution, the average unbanked worker spends an estimated $40,000 throughout his or her life just to cash paychecks. Unbanked and underbanked individuals may also fall prey to short-term, high-interest "payday" loans offered at check cashing outlets and other fringe financial institutions, becoming trapped in endless cycles of debt.[6]

In addition to the high individual cost associated with the use of fringe financial services, local economies suffer when residents are financially unstable. Communities in which a large proportion of households are struggling through financial crises confront greater needs and face the negative consequences of a cash economy, including eroded public safety due to increased theft and related crimes.[7]

### Why are People Unbanked?

There are many reasons why individuals do not have transactional accounts in a financial institution, or opt to use alternative financial services even if they do have one. The FDIC survey identified some common reasons:[8]

- High costs or perceived high cost: Many individuals believe they do not have enough money to maintain an account and are often deterred by "hidden" fees such as high minimum balance requirements, monthly service charges, and overdraft fees.

- Convenience: Banks and credit unions are often not accessible to low-income individuals due to their limited hours of operation and the lack of branches in some low-income neighborhoods.

- Need for immediate access to funds: For residents that do not use direct deposit, depositing a check into a checking account can take several days to clear.

---

4  FDIC 2009.

5  Barr, Michael S. 2004. "Banking the Poor: Policies to Bring Low-Income Americans into the Financial Mainstream." Washington DC: The Brookings Institution. Available at: http://www.brookings.edu/~/media/Files/rc/reports/2004/10childrenfamilies_barr/20041001_Banking.pdf.

6  Fellowes, Matt and M. Mabanta. 2008. "Banking on Wealth: America's New Retail Banking Infrastructure and Its Wealth-Building Potential." Washington DC: The Brookings Institution, Metropolitan Policy Program. Available at: http://www.brookings.edu/reports/2008/01_banking_fellowes.aspx.

7  Dreier, Peter, John Mollenkopf, and Todd Swanstrom. 2004. Second Edition, Revised. *Place Matters: Metropolitics for the Twenty-first Century.* Lawrence, KS: University Press of Kansas.; see also: Kubrin, Charis, Gregory D. Squires, & Steven M. Graves. "Does Fringe Banking Exacerbate Neighborhood and Crime Rates? Social Disorganization and the Ecology of Payday Lending." September 2009. Working Paper.

8  FDIC 2009.

- Lack of knowledge: Many individuals lack sufficient financial knowledge to navigate through the often complicated mainstream financial system.

- Identification requirements: Residents may believe they cannot open an account because they do not have a state issued driver's license

- Previous banking problems: Individuals may be barred from opening an account due to mistakes they made in previous banking relationships.

- Overall perceptions of banking: Many low-income residents hold a general belief that banks are not for them.

Who are the Unbanked?

The unbanked population is diverse, with different groups facing their own unique barriers to entering the financial mainstream. The section below describes the largest, most underserved segments of the unbanked population.

*Low-Income Households*

Low-income households comprise a large proportion of the unbanked population. Approximately 71 percent of unbanked households have annual earnings below $30,000.[9] Many low-income individuals distrust or are unfamiliar with mainstream financial institutions and instead use costly alternative financial services. Mainstream financial service providers often fail to meet the needs of low-income consumers. Low-income neighborhoods often have fewer mainstream banks or credit unions, and families may face transportation barriers in travelling to more distant branches. Financial institutions' hours of operation also pose challenges to low-income workers who often cannot leave their jobs midday to conduct financial transactions.

*Minority Households*

Minorities are more likely to be unbanked than white Americans. Black households (an estimated 21.7 percent) are most likely to be unbanked, followed by Hispanics (19.3 percent), and American Indians/Alaskans (15.6 percent). Overall, almost 54 percent of black households, 44.5 percent of American Indian/Alaskan households, and 43.3 percent of Hispanic households are either unbanked or underbanked.[10] There is a high correlation between low-income and minority groups it is therefore not surprising that minority groups face some of the same barriers to mainstream banking as low-income households, including intergenerational mistrust or negative experiences with banks.

*Immigrants*

Only 63 percent of immigrant heads of household have a checking account compared to 76 percent of native-born household heads. This number accounts for immigrants from all countries. Latin American immigrants are the most likely to be unbanked or underbanked. Just 27 percent of Mexican and 34 percent of El Salvadoran heads of households have a checking account compared to 48 percent of Chinese immigrant heads of households, and 72 percent of German immigrant household heads.[11]

Many immigrant groups face similar challenges in attaining accounts, including limited English proficiency and communication barriers, distrust of banks due to weak institutions in their country of origin, and the tendency to locate in immigrant enclaves, which can create unique cultural orientations toward alternative financial institutions.[12]

---

9 FDIC 2009.

10 FDIC 2009. Note that the terms, "black,""white," "Hispanic," and "American Indian/Alaskan" are those used in the FDIC document.

11 "Financial Access for Immigrants: Lessons From Diverse Perspectives." 2006. Chicago Federal Reserve Board & The Brookings Institution. Available at: http://www.brookings.edu/metro/pubs/20060504_financialaccess.pdf

12 FDIC 2009.

Banking on Opportunity
A Scan of the Evolving Field of Bank On Initiatives        US DEPARTMENT OF THE TREASURY        9
Office of Financial Education and Financial Access

In addition, immigrants often face real or perceived barriers to opening a bank or credit union account due to various identification requirements. According to the FDIC, almost all financial institutions require some form of government-issued identification, such as a driver's license or passport, to open a new account. Only 27 percent of banks accept the Mexican Matricula Consular card, which is an identity card issued by Mexican consulates to their citizens living abroad. The card allows the Mexican government to offer identification for its citizens while also keeping a record of their country of residence.[13] Thirty-eight percent of financial institutions accept Individual Taxpayer Identification Numbers (ITINs) instead of a Social Security Number.[14] An ITIN is a tax processing number issued by the Internal Revenue Service (IRS) to individuals, both resident and nonresident aliens, who need a U.S. taxpayer identification number to facilitate paying taxes but are not eligible for a Social Security Number (SSN).[15]

Immigrants also have distinct financial needs, most notably low-cost remittance products that enable them to send money back to relatives in their home countries. In 2004, Latin American and Caribbean immigrants sent a total of $34 billion in remittances to their home countries at a cost of approximately $2.4 billion in fees, and more than 40 percent of all immigrants remit money to their countries of origin.[16] Annual remittances have only climbed in the years following, with Latin American and Caribbean migrants sending $58.8 billion to their home region in 2009.[17]

Muslim immigrant groups and native-born Muslims may also face barriers to accessing mainstream financial products due to cultural prohibitions on the payment or acceptance of interest for borrowing and lending money. Because of these standards, some residents may not take advantage of interest-bearing accounts or loans offered by financial institutions.

*Individuals with Negative Banking Histories*

Many unbanked individuals have made financial mistakes or had negative experiences with financial institutions in the past. Nearly 8.3 percent of unbanked households have had problematic banking histories, such as overdrafts or poor credit.[18] These individuals are likely to have been reported to ChexSystems, a national database for banks that provides information based on check verifications about a potential customer's banking history. Financial institutions use ChexSystems primarily to identify people who have had past problems with accounts.

Most financial institutions have policies against opening accounts for individuals placed on the ChexSystems list. While individuals on ChexSystems may have had previous difficulties in managing a checking account, such as multiple overdrafts, the offense may have been unwitting. In some cases, the offense occurred in the distant past and access to safe, appropriate financial products and financial education can provide a fresh start for individuals who would become good customers. According to Fidelity National Information Services, Inc. (FIS), the company that owns the database, a ChexSystems record lasts for five years.[19] Financial institutions are under no obligation to report that customers have "settled up" their accounts or to request the removal of a negative report from the system. Therefore, customers may be affected by a report to ChexSystems for the full five years, even if they have paid any outstanding balances.

According to the FDIC, 87 percent of banks use a third party customer screening device such as ChexSystems when

13  "Consular ID Cards: Mexico and Beyond." 2003. Migration Policy Institute.

14  FDIC 2009.

15  "General ITIN Information." 2010. Washington DC: Internal Revenue Service.

16  FDIC 2009.

17  "Ten Years of Innovation in Remittances: Lessons Learned and Models for the Future." Access at http://idbdocs.iadb.org/wsdocs/getdocument.aspx?docnum=35163520

18  FDIC 2009.

19  Interview with FIS, Inc. staff. April 2011. More information about FIS, Inc. available at: http://www.fisglobal.com/index.htm.

10   **US DEPARTMENT OF THE TREASURY**
Office of Financial Education and Financial Access    Banking on Opportunity
A Scan of the Evolving Field of Bank On Initiatives

opening new accounts. Twenty-five percent of banks surveyed automatically reject a new account application that receives a negative screening result at the branch location. Of those institutions, only 49 percent are able to override a negative result on site while a customer is trying to open a new account. Just 25 percent of banks offer some type of second chance account designed for individuals who cannot qualify for a traditional account due to negative banking histories.[20]

## The Growing Field of Financial Access

A number of new research studies published over the last few years describe the size and characteristics of the unbanked market and the patterns of reliance that unbanked and underbanked consumers have on loosely regulated, fringe financial service providers to meet their transaction needs.[21]  This information – in addition to the prominence of the subprime mortgage and foreclosure crisis – has increased the visibility of financial access issues in the media and among nonprofits and policymakers at all levels of government.  It has also led to an increase in efforts to educate and protect consumers and expand access to an array of safe and affordable financial services, particularly for low-income households and communities of color.

This section provides a brief overview of some of the major efforts that have served to anchor and expand financial access in the U.S. We also briefly describe several basic models of banking access efforts that have taken place over the past decade before turning our attention to the details of the Bank On model for the remainder of the paper.[22]

### Financial Access Approaches

There have been various approaches to expanding financial access in the U.S. over the past several decades.  One strand has to do with reducing discrimination via financial service providers and expanding access to credit among low-income communities and communities of color.  To this end, the Community Reinvestment Act of 1977 was put in place to ensure that banks met the credit needs of the communities where they operate.

Other laws are also intended promote the availability of fairly priced credit in traditionally underserved communities. The Home Mortgage Disclosure Act (HMDA) passed in 1975 requires financial institutions to maintain and annually disclose data concerning home purchases, pre-approvals, home improvements, and refinance applications.[23]  This information is used by the public and by regulators to identify possible discriminatory lending patterns. The Equal Credit Opportunity Act (ECOA) prohibits discrimination in any aspect of a consumer or commercial credit transaction based on race, color, religion, national origin, sex, marital status, age, receipt of income from any public assistance program or the exercise, in good faith, of any right under the Consumer Credit Protection Act. The Fair Housing Act (FHA) prohibits discrimination based on race, color, religion, national origin, sex, familial status, or handicap, in all aspects of residential real estate transactions, including, but not limited to the sale, retail, appraisal, and financing of dwellings.[24]

Another approach has been to expand the availability of credit and financial services through creating and growing financial institutions with missions of serving underserved communities.  Early community development banking efforts such as the creation of South Shore Bank in Chicago in 1973, were also inspired by the idea that providing

---

20  FDIC 2009.

21  See for example:  FDIC 2009; *2008 CFSI Underbanked Consumer Study*; Fellowes, Matt and M. Mabanta. 2008. "Banking on Wealth: America's New Retail Banking Infrastructure and Its Wealth-Building Potential." Washington DC: The Brookings Institution, Metropolitan Policy Program.

22  A more in-depth overview of early policy initiatives to help the unbanked can be found in John P. Caskey et. al. 2004. "The Unbanked in Mexico and the United States."

23  http://www.fdic.gov/regulations/laws/rules/6500-3030.html#6500hmda1975.

24  http://www.fdic.gov/consumers/community/program.html.

Banking on Opportunity
A Scan of the Evolving Field of Bank On Initiatives      US DEPARTMENT OF THE TREASURY    11
Office of Financial Education and Financial Access

access to fairly priced capital for housing and business development in low-income communities and communities of color could not only be profitable but could help stabilize and revitalize these communities. Many such institutions are now considered community development financial institutions (CDFIs). A CDFI is a specialized, mission-driven financial institution that works in communities underserved by traditional financial institutions. CDFIs can be regulated institutions (banks and credit unions) and non-regulated institutions such as loan funds and venture capital funds. CDFIs provide a range of financial products and services in economically distressed markets, such as mortgage financing for low-income and first-time homebuyers and not-for-profit developers, flexible underwriting and risk capital for needed community facilities, and technical assistance, commercial loans and investments to small start-up or expanding businesses in low-income areas.

Among these mission-focused institutions are community-based financial institutions that have long existed to serve their communities with basic transaction and savings products, and credit. These include for-profit community banks, and credit unions, which are member-owned not-for-profit financial institutions. For example, many community development credit unions (CDCUs) have operated in Black or African American communities for decades, accepting deposits, cashing checks, making loans, issuing credit cards and providing other financial services.

## Financial Access Models

### First Accounts

In 2002, the U.S. Department of the Treasury launched the First Accounts program to increase access to financial services among low- and moderate-income individuals (LMI)[25] without bank or credit union accounts through the development of appropriate and replicable financial products and services, including financial education. The Treasury Department funded 15 organizations, including financial institutions, community-based non-profit organizations and one local government agency to develop or expand projects designed to provide low-cost checking or savings accounts. Over the course of two years, the First Accounts initiative facilitated access to accounts for more than 37,000 previously unbanked individuals.[26]

### Alliances for Economic Inclusion

In 2006, FDIC Chairman Sheila Bair created the Advisory Committee on Economic Inclusion to explore ways of bringing the unbanked into the financial mainstream. In 2007, the initiative was further expanded through the launch of regional Alliances for Economic Inclusion (AEI). These broad-based coalitions of financial institutions, community-based organizations and other partners in communities across the country were supported by the FDIC with the goal of expanding the availability of basic financial products and services – including savings accounts, affordable remittance products, small-dollar loan programs, targeted financial education programs, alternative delivery channels and other asset-building programs – for underserved populations. For example, the AEI in the Gulf Coast region has focused on financial services gaps as well as hurricane recovery initiatives. The Gulf Coast coalition has 70 members and three subcommittees that have been working to: 1) create a mortgage program with alternative underwriting that can be used for the rehabilitation of hurricane-damaged homes, the refinancing of predatory mortgages, and foreclosure prevention; 2) increase the awareness and usage of the free Volunteer Income Tax Assistance (VITA) service and link more LMI taxpayers to savings opportunities; and 3) develop strategies to help small businesses recover through the development of special loan pools, technical assistance services and neighborhood small business information fairs.[27]

---

25 Defined as a family income that does not exceed—(1) for nonmetropolitan areas, 80 percent of the statewide median family income; or (2) for metropolitan areas, 80 percent of the greater of the statewide median family income or metropolitan area median family income.

26 "Findings from the First Accounts Program." 2009. Washington DC: U.S. Department of the Treasury.

27 "AEI Regional Initiatives - Memphis Area Office." FDIC. Available at: http://www.fdic.gov/consumers/community/AEI/regional/memphis.html

As of January 2011, there are 15 AEI coalitions located in the following areas[28]:

* Black Belt Counties, AL[29]
* Boston, MA
* Worcester, MA
* Chicago, IL
* Detroit/South Michigan, MI
* Milwaukee, WI
* South Texas, TX[30]
* Kansas City, KS/MO
* New Orleans/Southeast Louisiana, LA
* Mississippi Gulf Coast, MS
* Little Rock, AR
* Baltimore, MD
* Wilmington, DE
* Rochester, NY
* Los Angeles, CA

AEI communities in which the FDIC has provided assistance in the launch or maintenance of Bank On campaigns include: Houston, TX (as part of South Texas AEI); Los Angeles, CA; Detroit, MI; and Bank On Central Texas, based in Austin.

*Community Financial Access Pilot*

In 2008, the Treasury Department launched the Community Financial Access Pilot (CFAP) in which Treasury Department officials worked with eight communities to increase the availability of financial education and mainstream financial services for underserved populations. The approaches used by local pilot sites varied substantially in accordance to each community's respective needs, priorities and resources. Three of the pilot sites – Philadelphia, PA, Fresno, CA, and Cowlitz County, WA – implemented Bank On initiatives to meet CFAP goals. A fourth pilot site, Jacksonville, FL, built on its Fresh Start Accounts project through the CFAP to eventually develop Bank On Jacksonville. The CFAP included in-depth professional assistance to each site provided by two community consultants, without grant funding.[31]

*New York City Office of Financial Empowerment*

New York City's Office of Financial Empowerment (OFE) was developed in 2006 as the first local government entity focused on educating, empowering, and protecting low-income residents in order to enable them to become more financially stable. OFE has piloted several innovative financial access programs. In 2010, building on their Opportunity NYC Basic Account Pilot, OFE created the NYC SafeStart Account. The city partnered with five banks and five credit unions to offer this starter account exclusively to clients at the city's Financial Empowerment Centers. The account, which provides only an ATM card, does not have overdraft or monthly fees (provided that the minimum balance requirement of $25 is met).

Further, New York City's OFE has also partnered with San Francisco as co-chairs of Cities for Financial Empowerment (CFE), a coalition of local governments in cities across the U.S. dedicated to advancing innovative

---

28  http://www.fdic.gov/consumers/community/AEI/index.html.

29  The FDIC defines the Black Belt to include the counties of Barbour, Bullock, Butler, Choctaw, Clarke, Conecuh, Dallas, Escambia, Greene, Hale, Lowndes, Macon, Marengo, Monroe, Perry, Pickens, Sumter, Washington and Wilcox. The two adjoining Gulf Coast hurricane-impacted counties of Mobile and Baldwin, AL are also included in AEI efforts.

30  Primarily the cities of Austin, Houston, and San Antonio.

31  More information about the CFAP project is available at www.treasury.gov/cfap.

Banking on Opportunity
A Scan of the Evolving Field of Bank On Initiatives | US DEPARTMENT OF THE TREASURY | 13
Office of Financial Education and Financial Access

financial empowerment initiatives as a means to improve the financial health of their residents. By expanding the vision of how municipal government can serve its citizens and create pathways for financial stability, CFE leverages politics in the service of at-risk communities, and provides a platform for cities to work and learn collectively, forging partnerships with public, private, and non-profit sectors. Besides the co-chairs, CFE member cities, as of early 2011, include Chicago, County of Hawai'i, Los Angeles, Miami, Newark, Providence, San Antonio, Savannah, and Seattle.[32]

Campaigns that Promote Savings and Financial Access

The formation of AEIs and Bank On was happening at the same time when many state coalitions that had traditionally focused their advocacy efforts on expanding access to the federal Earned Income Tax Credit (EITC) or helping low-income families build assets began to get engaged in financial access issues. The large number of state and local tax coalitions around the country provided a natural infrastructure for stakeholders to begin raising residents' awareness about the importance of protecting assets through a banking relationship or other type of financial service or product. Many states and cities started focusing on the issue in their existing asset-building coalitions. In Baltimore, MD, for example, the local asset-building organization, Baltimore CASH Campaign, was and continues to be a key player in the city's financial access efforts, including tax time opportunities to open bank accounts and build assets.

In addition, the issue of financial access became more prominent through national campaigns that began highlighting the need to connect unbanked and underbanked residents with safe, affordable financial products in order to ensure these residents' short- and long-term financial stability. America Saves is a nationwide campaign managed by the Consumer Federation of America that works to build broad coalitions across the country of nonprofit, corporate, and government groups to help individuals and families save and build wealth. In a growing number of states and communities, these coalitions have organized and maintain local America Saves campaigns with various partners, structures and activities. In general, the campaigns offer residents access to a variety of web-based tools and other resources, such as workshops and financial planners, to equip them in learning how to save and build assets The campaigns also facilitate access, through financial institution partnerships, to affordable savings accounts and other financial products. There are approximately 60 state and local America Saves campaigns at various stages of development throughout the country.[33]

*Bank On San Francisco*

In 2005, the City and County of San Francisco began work on Bank On San Francisco, in partnership with the New America Foundation, Earned Assets Resource Network (EARN), the Federal Reserve Bank of San Francisco and 15 banks and credit unions. Bank On San Francisco was the first municipal program in the nation to address the needs of unbanked residents by actively moving the marketplace to offer financial products and services that are suitable for lower-income consumers. By developing an innovative partnership that draws on the strengths of government agencies, banks and credit unions, and a wide range of community partners, Bank On San Francisco partners united around the ambitious goal to bank 10,000 unbanked San Franciscans in two years. The pilot program was launched in September 2006. In its first five years, Bank On San Francisco opened more than 70,000 checking accounts for formerly unbanked individuals.

Emergence and Growth of the Bank On Field

Municipal leaders in San Francisco first began developing the Bank On model in 2005. At that time, city leaders were noticing that the many of the families receiving the city's new local Earned Income Tax Credit, the Working Families Credit, did not have an account with a bank or credit union in which to directly deposit their refund. The

---

32  More information about CFE is available at its website www.cfecoalition.org.

33  "America Saves: About Us." Available at: http://www.americasaves.org/about/.

Brookings Institution conducted research to further examine this issue and found that an estimated one in five San Franciscans, and half of the city's Blacks/African-Americans and Hispanics/Latinos, did not have accounts and were paying 2 to 5 percent of their incomes to cash their paychecks.

In response, Mayor Gavin Newsom and City Treasurer José Cisneros invited financial institutions to join the city, the Federal Reserve Bank of San Francisco, and community-based nonprofit partners to create and launch Bank On San Francisco. The program would offer low- income residents alternatives to check-cashing outlets by increasing the supply of starter accounts that provided easy, affordable ways to deposit paychecks, pay bills, and save.

The city launched Bank On San Francisco in September 2006 after over a year of development by a coalition of city officials, 15 banks and credit unions, the Federal Reserve Bank of San Francisco, and a large number of community organizations. The program had a goal to bank 10,000 unbanked San Franciscans in two years. By the following year, the program surpassed its own expectations, with 11,110 previously unbanked San Franciscans acquiring accounts through the program.

Following San Francisco's lead, cities, counties, and states adopted the Bank On concept as a model for promoting access to mainstream financial services, supporting working families, and strengthening local economies. The program appeals to local leaders due to its replicable nature and its relatively low costs. Many of the communities that launched Bank On programs already had established key partnerships with financial institutions and community organizations resulting from other asset-building efforts, including EITC outreach campaigns, savings campaigns like America Saves or MoneySmart Week, asset-building coalitions and the FDIC's Alliance for Economic Inclusion (AEI) coalitions.

Many government agencies and nongovernmental organizations have worked directly with community leaders to help them develop Bank On initiatives. In response to the growing interest among municipal leaders in helping residents connect to the financial mainstream, NLC's Institute for Youth, Education and Families launched the Bank On Cities Campaign in early 2008. The campaign was designed to help local elected officials and their senior staff in 18 cities replicate the Bank On San Francisco model over a two-year period. Cities were encouraged to collaborate with financial institutions and community-based organizations to provide LMI residents with access to basic, low-cost financial services. The campaign also helped municipal officials develop and advance more comprehensive, local asset-building and asset-protection agendas to help families achieve financial stability.

Between 2007 and 2010, NLC partnered with the City and County of San Francisco to provide technical assistance to nearly 75 cities seeking to replicate the Bank On model. NLC also partnered with San Francisco officials to launch the www. joinbankon.org web portal to streamline access to information and resources for emerging Bank On programs. In 2008, under Governor Schwarzenegger's leadership, California became the first state to launch a Bank On initiative. A number of the state's largest cities and financial institutions, along with United Way chapters and other partners, agreed to support the opening of accounts meeting minimum standards, provide financial education, and form coalitions to market the accounts.

## Geographic Variation of Bank On Programs

Although Bank On initiatives are most commonly led by local governments, a few states, counties, and regions have also sought to develop initiatives that cover a broader geographic area. Various state and regional entities such as governor's offices, state treasurers, and regional nonprofit organizations have led these efforts.

Regional efforts may focus on a county or several cities and towns within a state. For example, Bank On Central Texas, led by the United Way of Central Texas, encompasses Austin and the regional/metro area served by that United Way. Also in Texas, the Bank On Bryan program developed by the City of Bryan evolved into a regional Bank On Brazos Valley initiative. During the program development phase, it became clear that Bryan's sister city, College Station, should be included since financial institution and other community partners served both cities equally.

Banking on Opportunity
A Scan of the Evolving Field of Bank On Initiatives    US DEPARTMENT OF THE TREASURY    15
Office of Financial Education and Financial Access

Statewide Bank On programs began to emerge beginning with the launch of Bank On California in 2008. A state government official such as a governor or state treasurer usually leads these statewide efforts. The goal of statewide programs so far has been to act as an umbrella effort to coordinate and help strengthen local initiatives within the state. There are currently statewide Bank On initiatives in California, Indiana, Illinois, and Florida. With the exception of Illinois, these programs were developed following the launch of one or two city-based programs.

Statewide initiatives typically coordinate some of the primary tasks associated with developing a Bank On initiative, such as financial institution involvement and financial product negotiation. In some cases, financial institutions prefer to offer a common Bank On account across all local programs within a state rather than negotiating with each individual community.

A state program can bolster local efforts in other ways. State legislators can advocate for policies that protect consumers and expand access to mainstream financial services. Officials in state departments, such as a treasurer's office or banking department, can provide guidance and information to local programs. Statewide initiatives also have the potential to be especially useful in rural areas. Small, rural cities and towns often do not have the infrastructure necessary to build a program on their own. There may not be a diverse set of financial institutions within the local area, or there may be few community organizations with the capacity to conduct outreach or offer financial education to participants. A state program can offer resources to help programs in rural areas get off the ground.

## The Bank On Model

The Bank On model is driven by partnerships. Municipal leaders, community organizations, financial institutions, and other community stakeholders work together to create pathways to safe, affordable financial services for unbanked and underbanked individuals. Bank On programs increase the supply of "starter account products" by developing baseline criteria for Bank On products that participating financial institutions agree to offer, inform unbanked consumers about the benefits of account ownership and encourage them to open accounts, and raise community-wide awareness of the risks associated with being unbanked. Important Bank On goals include decreasing reliance on check cashers, payday lenders, and other predatory financial services and making high-quality money management education more easily available to underserved populations.

A typical Bank On financial product may include the following features:

* A low- or no-cost checking account;
* A low or no minimum monthly balance;
* Forgiveness of certain charges related to non-sufficient funds or overdrafts;
* Flexibility in opening accounts for individuals in ChexSystems; and
* Acceptance of alternative forms of identification as primary identification, such as the Mexican Matricula Consular card.

Bank On programs also typically include a financial education component in order to help participants better manage their accounts and achieve and maintain financial stability.

While none of the Bank On program leaders responding to the NLC survey require remittance products to be offered as part of their overall product suite, some programs have encouraged participating financial institutions to offer remittance opportunities to Bank On customers.[34]   For example, Bank On Houston requires that participating financial institutions offer at least one "additional" product feature beyond the standard criteria, with the provision of remittance products as a suggested way to satisfy this requirement. Similarly, most financial institutions participating in Bank On Florida offer a remittance product.

---

34 "National Survey of Bank On Programs." 2010. Washington DC: National League of Cities.

Through marketing and outreach campaigns, program leaders inform residents about the new financial products and services that are available. Marketing messages not only encourage use of the product, but also incorporate general public service messages about the importance of saving and keeping money safe. Community-based organization partners play a key role in conducting outreach to targeted, underserved populations that many financial institutions do not often reach through their own advertising.

## The Bank On Landscape Today

Since Bank On San Francisco was launched in 2006, efforts to replicate the model have spread across the country. Based on data collected by NLC as of April 2011, 32 cities, four states, and two regions have fully implemented Bank On initiatives.

In 2007, Seattle became the first community to replicate the San Francisco model by launching Bank On Seattle-King County, and in 2008, two more community programs (Evansville, IN, and Los Angeles) and the first state program (Bank On California) were launched. As news of early program successes spread, more localities and states developed Bank On initiatives, with 10 new programs launched in 2009 and 13 more in 2010. In the first quarter of 2011, four more programs were launched. The four existing statewide programs were developed over a similar time frame as the city initiatives. After the launch of Bank On California in December 2008, Indiana and Illinois followed in 2009 and Bank On Florida in 2010. See the appendix for more information.

It generally takes local partners between six and 18 months to develop a Bank On initiative from an initial idea to a fully implemented program. By the summer of 2012, an estimated 20 additional programs that are now in development are likely to be launched. More efforts that are underway are in earlier stages of development, as local leaders that have expressed interest in the idea and are just beginning to plan.

### Program Leadership and Staffing

Bank On programs benefit from strong leadership provided by local or state government leaders. Local governments have been engaged in most Bank On program developed to date and play a lead coordinating role in most programs. Some efforts are jointly led by the city and a community partner. Many Bank On initiatives are created when a local elected official – most often a mayor, city councilmember, or a city treasurer – champions the program and establishes a steering committee for developing the program. City staff and coalition partners often carry out the day-to-day tasks.

In some cases, a mayor and treasurer or a mayor and councilmember pair up to support the program, and each plays a different role in building public support for the program. For example, in Houston, then-City Controller Annise Parker, who is now mayor, played a lead role in bringing the Bank On concept to her city and coordinating efforts, while then-Mayor Bill White supported the initiative and used his "bully pulpit" to build public support. According to NLC's survey, a community entity, such as a United Way or an asset-building coalition, acts as the primary coordinator for about 15 percent of programs. For 87 percent of Bank On initiatives, one or more staff from a city agency or community organization dedicates a portion of their hours to managing the program. Others rely on volunteers or hire consultants to manage program development.

### Partnerships

Each Bank On partner plays a unique role in program development and implementation. Because of the nature of the model, no one entity could create and manage a Bank On program on its own. Typical partners in a Bank On initiative include municipal staff, federal regulatory agencies, nonprofit or community-based organization staff, and bank or credit union representatives. Some programs have also engaged different partners depending on specific community circumstances and needs. A varied set of partner organizations can help Bank On programs reach diverse segments of the population. The following four key partners have been part of every Bank On program launched thus far, according to information gathered for NLC's survey.

Banking on Opportunity
A Scan of the Evolving Field of Bank On Initiatives     US DEPARTMENT OF THE TREASURY     17
Office of Financial Education and Financial Access

## Local Government

Local elected officials play an influential role in convening partners, uniting stakeholders around a common agenda, negotiating with financial institutions, enlisting community organizations, and generating publicity for a Bank On program. Local officials can designate staff from different city agencies to oversee development of the program. For example, in Indianapolis, City Neighborhood Liaisons provide information about Bank On Indy to underserved residents in low-income neighborhoods, subsidized housing developments and correctional facilities. The City of Bryan, TX utilized its media department to help Bank On Brazos Valley develop public service announcements to reach target audiences through popular local radio stations. Moreover, city leaders can gain the support of financial institutions and negotiate product development by leveraging the business relationship cities have as customers with large amounts of assets in local banks.

## Financial Institutions

Banks and credit unions are vital partners as the main point of delivery for a Bank On account. Financial institutions also have the expertise necessary in financial products and services to help other partners formulate a product strategy. Financial institution representatives who participate in the development of a Bank On initiative work in various departments which may include regional leadership teams, community development staff, or branch managers.

Financial institution partners usually include a combination of large national banks, community and regional banks, credit unions and CDFIs. Bank On initiatives usually have a total of between eight and 12 financial institution partners, engaging between one and five of each type of institutions. Large banks are the most common partner for Bank On programs, perhaps because of their significant presence within communities and their ability to provide larger financial contributions to programs.

Fewer Bank On programs reported involvement of CDFI partners. About 60 percent of programs engage one or more CDFIs while almost 40 percent of programs reported that they were not working with a CDFI. This relatively lower participation could be explained by the absence of CDFIs from some of the Bank On communities or that many CDFIs are loan funds which do not have the ability to offer retail financial products or transactional accounts.

To date, only one Bank On initiative is known to include a non-bank pre-paid debit card provider. Bank on Central Texas collaborates with Mango Financial, to give participants the option of a prepaid Mastercard-branded debit card, which provides users account access through mobile phone or internet, rather than a physical financial institution location.

## Community Groups/Non-Profit Organizations

Nonprofit community organizations such as local United Ways, faith-based organizations, neighborhood groups, and financial education providers are often most connected to unbanked and underbanked communities and provide important insights that help programs meet the needs of the target population. These partners are often seen as trusted messengers, facilitating outreach to unbanked residents. Community groups frequently serve as the program's fiscal agent, receiving and managing any funding associated with the program. Although community groups usually work closely with city program leaders, NLC found that community organizations played a lead role in coordinating about 15 percent of Bank On initiatives.

In addition, other partners in the community that have supported Bank On programs include local universities, advocates for people with disabilities, utility companies, media partners (such as Univision and other ethnic media outlets), local businesses, police officers, former local elected officials, marketing firms, and state officials. For example, in Dallas, the police department has played a strong role in Bank On outreach because the department views financial access as an important public safety issue. In another example of creative partnerships, Bank On Fresno leaders worked with the Spanish-language television and media company, Univision, to create several public service announcements and vignettes that promoted the program and the importance of financial education to Spanish-speaking residents.

Universities have been an asset to several Bank On initiatives, providing expertise in research, financial education and other key aspects of the program. For example, before designing Bank On Savannah, program planners worked with Savannah State University to assess the local financial landscape and learn how residents were using banks and alternative financial service outlets. In Indianapolis, the Bank On Indy tracking committee partnered with Indiana University and Purdue University on a performance measurement project to improve the program's data tracking and evaluation process.

### Financial Regulators

Federal financial regulators have proven to be essential partners in Bank On initiatives. The Federal Reserve Bank of San Francisco played a key role in the creation of the first Bank On initiative. Community affairs officers in various Federal Reserve Banks, the Federal Deposit Insurance Corporation (FDIC) and the Office of the Comptroller of the Currency (OCC) have supported other local Bank On initiatives by providing guidance on financial product development and banking practices and by helping engage and convene financial institution representatives. Regulatory partners have also helped conduct preliminary research on community needs, and offered their general expertise, experience, and credibility in working with financial institutions to assist underserved markets. Finally, regulatory partners act as data repositories by collecting program data from financial institutions and sharing it with other program partners. According to NLC's survey, federal regulators are involved in 90 percent of Bank On programs. About three-quarters of programs partner with regional Federal Reserve Banks and almost 70 percent partner with regional FDIC community affairs offices.

Some programs, such as Bank On Manhattan and Bank On Seattle-King County, also partner with state financial regulators. The Washington Department of Financial Institutions (DFI) is a co-sponsor of Bank On Seattle-King County and has been involved with the development and implementation of the program. Washington DFI also tracks and collects program data from participating financial institutions. The New York State Banking Department (NYSBD) co-hosted Bank On Manhattan's initial meetings and participates in its steering committee. NYSBD also helped the program negotiate Bank On Manhattan's baseline product features.

### Budgets and Funding

Bank On initiatives have not had large budgets for their activities. Budgets vary widely in scope depending on the region and details of the program. Initiatives have pieced together limited funds, donated resources, and in-kind staff from government departments and community organizations, for example. Funds are predominantly spent on marketing materials, including design, billboard ads, bus cards, flyers, brochures, buckslips,[35] window clings for financial institution branches, and a variety of other products. Other costs include contracts for services from commercial firms (e.g., for marketing or research) and/or nonprofit organizations (e.g., for fiscal agent services, financial education, etc.). Most programs spend less than 25 percent of their budgets on staffing. About 40 percent of respondents to NLC's survey reported budgets of $25,000 or less, while 20 percent have budgets of more than $100,000. Bank On initiatives are funded through a combination of donated and in-kind services and resources, financial contributions from participating financial institutions, contributions at fundraising events and occasionally grant funding or cities' general funds.[36]

Contributions from financial institutions are generally based on a formula that incorporates bank or credit union size

---

35 Buckslips are slips of paper the size of a dollar bill, often inserted into direct mail campaigns.
36 The city general fund covers activities not accounted for in other line items or grants. Most tax-funded functions – such as police and fire protection – are funded from a city's general fund. The revenues contributing to a general city fund typically are from taxes, utility fees, licenses, permits and inspection fees and fines. From: Bland, Robert L. and Irene S. Rubin. "Budgeting: A Guide for Local Governments." International City/County Management Association, Washington, D.C. 1997.

and the number of branches located in the designated community or a tiered sponsorship structure with institutions contributing at different sponsorship levels. Bank On initiatives also seek funding from local foundations, community organizations, government agencies, businesses and other partners to support the work.

Most initiatives budget for the first one to two years of operation and then conduct additional fundraising for longer-term marketing and outreach. After the first couple of years, programs typically do not require the same level of funding because many of the initial upfront costs, such as the development of the website or logo, are already in place. Program leaders also have a better sense of what marketing materials were most successful, which allows subsequent marketing campaigns to be more targeted. Bank On Indy, for example, was able to reduce program costs by finding more efficient ways of printing marketing materials and targeting specific populations instead of using mass marketing techniques. Because program leaders also secured donated billboards and bus cards, only production costs were incurred.

The cost of a Bank On program is often reduced by the donation of in-kind services and resources by local and national partners. For example, the City of San Francisco received pro bono marketing materials from a marketing firm and allowed those materials to be used by other Bank On initiatives free of charge. By sharing these materials, San Francisco leaders helped communities that took advantage of this offer significantly decrease the initial costs of their initiatives.

## Bank On Financial Product Features

A key foundational component of Bank On programs is the transaction account that is offered to unbanked consumers. Therefore, Bank On program leaders carefully negotiate the product criteria with financial institutions to ensure that they meet the needs of the target population. At the same time, participating financial institutions need to feel comfortable with a product that will meet their business needs.

Therefore, many Bank On programs have conducted initial research on the financial services needs of the community and identified existing products in participating financial institutions that are targeted toward underserved consumers. Financial institution and regulatory partners have also provided important feedback on product development.

Cities that have launched Bank On programs have developed similar baseline products, which typically adopt the following standard components based on the original Bank On San Francisco model:

| Product Feature | Percentage of programs responding to NLC's survey |
|---|---|
| No or low monthly fees (under $10)[37] | 100% |
| Low or no minimum monthly balance | 80% |
| Flexibility in opening accounts for individuals who have been in ChexSystems. | 80% |
| Ways to minimize overdraft fees[38] | 72% |
| Acceptance of alternative forms of identification, such as consular identification[39] | 69% |
| A savings account or other savings option | 47% |

---

37  "Low" monthly fees are not always defined by each individual Bank On program. However, typically they refer to fees that are less than $10.

38  These include forgiveness of a series of overdraft charges within the first year; the option to opt-in to overdraft protection (versus automatic enrollment); encouraging financial education to learn how to avoid overdraft charges and how much they can cost over time.

39  Financial institutions consider alternative identifications "strong" if it includes of layers of protections to ensure that the person using the card is in fact, the person he/she claims to be. This includes identifying items such as a photo, the address, date of birth, holograms, and other security mechanisms.

Some programs built on the standard Bank On product by adding other components that meet the specific needs of the unbanked and underbanked populations in their communities. For example, Bank On Newark offers customers one free money order per month as a feature of their baseline product because many local residents rely on money orders to pay their rent. Customers signing up for Bank On D.C. accounts would have to "opt in" for overdraft protection, rather than automatically being placed in the program. Other additional product components that some programs added to their basic accounts include:

- A free ATM or debit card;
- Clear and thorough disclosure of bank product features and policies;
- Free online banking; and
- Encouragement of direct deposit.

Access to safe, appropriate financial products and financial education can provide a fresh start for individuals who are in ChexSystems for reasons other than fraud, helping them become low-risk, sustainable accountholders. Bank On programs and other financial access initiatives have made it a priority to provide pathways to the financial mainstream for those in ChexSystems. Strategies have included mandating financial education before an individual on ChexSystems can open an account, flexible restitution policies, or provisions for opening accounts when individuals have a ChexSystems history that is more than six months old. According to NLC's Bank On survey, 80 percent of programs require that participating institutions provide options for individuals in ChexSystems as part of their baseline product.

## Financial Education

In today's constantly changing financial marketplace, people can choose from countless financial services options, many of which can be detrimental to individuals who lack the knowledge to navigate the financial system or have struggled with banking in the past. Bank On initiatives have addressed this issue by providing accessible financial education, which may also alleviate financial institutions' hesitation to reach out to unbanked individuals. Findings from the U.S. Department of the Treasury's CFAP report reinforce the importance of financial education in promoting the successful use of financial products and services.[40]

All respondents to NLC's survey have some type of financial education component within their Bank On programs. Most programs make financial education available to all Bank On customers but generally do not require financial education in order to obtain an account. However, some initiatives, such as the one in Cowlitz County, WA, require financial education for participants in the ChexSystems database who seek second chance or "fresh start" accounts. This requirement helps financial institutions feel more comfortable in offering accounts to this traditionally high-risk population. Some initiatives, such as Bank On San Francisco, only require financial education for those with a ChexSystems history that is less than a year old.

### Classes and Curricula

Typically, Bank On initiatives coordinate with existing financial education classes in the community and provide that information to participants. Bank On initiatives often develop a set of financial education standards that providers should meet, which cover important, basic banking and financial management concepts.

While most Bank On initiatives do not develop an independent financial education curriculum, a handful of communities have designed their own curricula to meet program goals. Bank On Evansville, IN leaders developed

---

40 "Community Financial Access Pilot Report." 2010. Washington DC: United States Department of the Treasury. Available at: http://www.treasury.gov/resource-center/financial-education/Documents/Community%20Financial%20Access%20Pilot%20Report.pdf.

Banking on Opportunity
A Scan of the Evolving Field of Bank On Initiatives        US DEPARTMENT OF THE TREASURY        21
Office of Financial Education and Financial Access

a financial education curriculum and complementary training guide for instructors that is targeted specifically toward Bank On customers. In Jacksonville, FL, program partners developed a special financial education curriculum for participants with a ChexSystems history. Bank On Jacksonville's financial education committee, working with the University of Florida and Duval County Cooperative Extension combined the Get Checking curriculum with relevant Money Smart modules to create "Fresh $tart Training." After successfully completing the one-day workshop, participants receive certificates that will allow them to open accounts at participating banks and credit unions.[41]

Many programs use a combination of existing financial education classes offered in the community and the FDIC's Money Smart curriculum. Money Smart is a comprehensive financial education curriculum designed to help LMI and financially underserved individuals enhance their financial skills and develop informed, positive relationships with banks and credit unions.[42]

Money Smart is widely used for a number of reasons, including its comprehensiveness, ease of use, and availability in multiple languages.

### Financial Education Delivery

In most Bank On initiatives, financial education is delivered in a classroom setting on a regular basis (typically weekly or monthly). Program partners strive to make educational opportunities available at times and locations that are convenient to participants. Bank On customers learn about financial education opportunities from financial institutions when they open accounts, or through relationships with community organizations, which either directly provide or refer to the financial education. Classes are also advertised on partner websites or in other community resource materials.

Encouraging attendance at financial education classes can be challenging because the lives of working families are often hectic. For some families, lack of transportation or child care pose barriers to participation. As a result, a few programs provide incentives for participating in financial education. For example, some financial institutions in Seattle-King County offer a $50 or $100 incentive for customers who attend classes. In one Bank On program in Illinois, financial education participants receive food vouchers from grocery stores and food pantries.

In a small number of programs, including Bank On San Francisco, one-on-one financial counseling or coaching is available to Bank On participants. This more intensive coaching method can more directly address participants' specific financial concerns and increase their financial capability in a more targeted way.

Web-based financial education has also gained attention. In Washington, DC, Bank On customers are encouraged to create profiles and participate in online, goal-based financial education. Bank on D.C partnered with Financial Education Literacy Advisors (FELA) to create an online portal that helps clients identify goals, interests and needs, measures learning outcomes, and connects clients with resources that help them achieve their personal financial goals.

### Marketing and Outreach Strategies

Thoughtful marketing and outreach strategies are necessary to inform the public about Bank On initiatives. In some communities, marketing campaigns also contain public service messages about the importance of using mainstream banking instead of high-cost alternative services and the benefits of saving and storing money in a

---

41  To learn more about Bank on Jacksonville and its Fresh $tart program, visit: http://www.bankonjacksonville.com/wp-content/uploads/2011/02/Fresh-Start-Brochure-121010.pdf.

42  More information about Money Smart is available on the FDIC's website: http://www.fdic.gov/consumers/consumer/moneysmart/.

safe place. Most communities designate a specific committee of Bank On partners to coordinate marketing and outreach. Some Bank On initiatives turn to communications firms to help coordinate their advertising campaigns. San Francisco laid the groundwork for many other Bank On initiatives' marketing efforts. The city received pro bono services from McCann Worldgroup, a large marketing firm that created all of the program's marketing materials. The city then made these materials available to other Bank On initiatives. To date, 28 Bank On programs have signed a Memorandum of Understanding (MOU) with the City and County of San Francisco to use these

materials in their marketing campaigns. The MOU requires programs to use the materials solely to promote a Banx On program that is consistent with the original model launched in San Francisco.

Bank On programs use a variety of materials and media to promote their products and services, including earned media (such as interviews on local radio programs), with marketing efforts often determined by the available budget. Local media outreach may involve public service announcements, op-eds in local newspapers, insertion in voter information guides, and sound bites on television and radio. Distribution of printed materials is often a large component of most Bank On marketing campaigns. Some Bank On campaigns have used outdoor marketing options such as billboards, bus ads, and posters placed in bus shelters and other public locations. The messages in these outreach materials reflect local needs. For example, San Francisco's marketing materials highlight the high costs of alternative financial services with advertisements that read, "Check Cashing Shrinks Your Paycheck. Now You Can Open a Bank Account."[43]

Fliers and buckslips are often made available at banks and community-based organizations and distributed to employers, affordable housing providers, city agencies, and other settings frequented by unbanked residents. Several communities, including St. Petersburg, FL, and Houston, TX have conducted direct mail campaigns with key partners such as the local utility company and school districts.

The majority of Bank On programs have websites that provide information about which financial institutions offer accounts, in addition to other information, such as sites offering financial education and counseling, and event calendars. Social marketing also seems o be an effective outreach strategy. For example, Bank On Fresno has combined traditional marketing and outreach strategies with use of social media – including Facebook, MySpace, Twitter and Mindhub – and

43  For more information, visit http://media.bankonsf.org/en/PDF/BankonSFCaseStudy.pdf.

Banking on Opportunity
A Scan of the Evolving Field of Bank On Initiatives          US DEPARTMENT OF THE TREASURY          23
Office of Financial Education and Financial Access

marketing through college campuses, Univision vignettes, and public service announcements in ten languages. Many communities use a local service referral phone line to provide callers with information about Bank On opportunities. These services include 211 lines run by the local United Way and 311 lines run by cities, which are designed to provide residents with general information about local public services. In Seattle-King County, Bank On program information is incorporated into the city's online public benefit screening tool, PeoplePoint. PeoplePoint offers service providers in multiple agencies a way to assess clients' eligibility for public benefits, including food stamps, health insurance, and utility assistance.

Service referral lines help cities assess the impact of their marketing campaigns. In San Francisco, referral line callers are asked how they heard about Bank On. The most frequent responses from residents that call the referral line are that they learned about the program through bus and billboard ads. In many cities, financial institutions also track referral mechanisms. The most common method of referrals reported by financial institutions is "word of mouth," including recommendations from people involved in community groups, churches and schools.

## Use of Technology

### Bank On Websites

Leaders of Bank On initiatives have used technology to enhance their programs in several ways. As mentioned above, almost all Bank On programs have a website to disseminate information to the public, potential customers, and partners. Some websites offer tools that customers can use to navigate the financial system. For example, several programs, including Bank On Denver and Bank On San Francisco, have a mapping tool, which can be used to search for financial institutions and products that meet certain criteria, such as location, monthly fees, and types of identification participating financial institutions will accept.

### Bank On Denver Mapping Tool

Bank On Denver leaders secured the assistance of a mapping design company, Maptive, to develop a mapping tool for the program's website. The tool helps customers identify the financial institution that matches search criteria for branch location, product offerings, and bank identification requirements. Below is a screen shot from the mapping tool.[44]

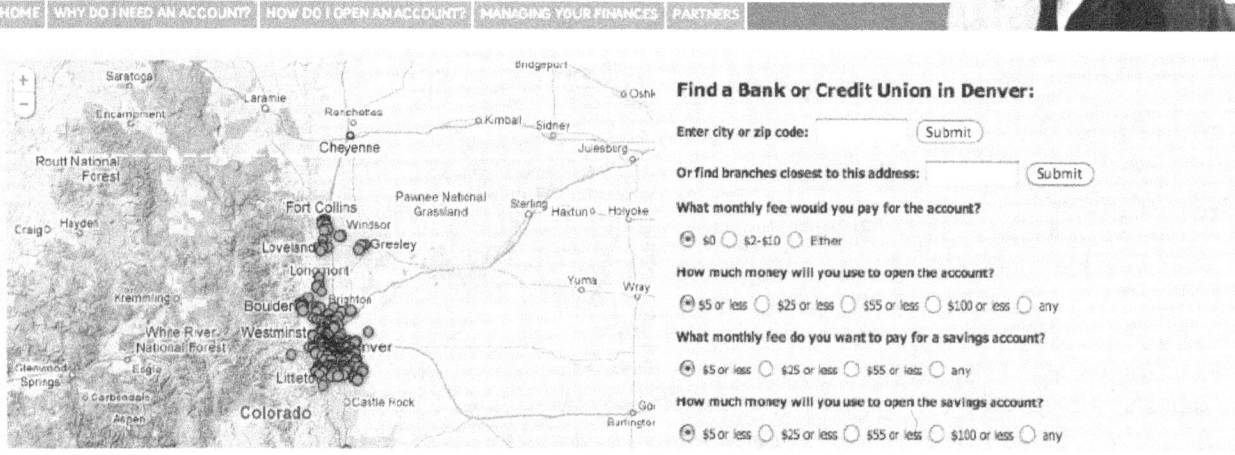

---

44 To view Denver's program locator tool, visit: http://www.bankondenver.org/map.

Bank On Philadelphia is among the programs that share marketing materials with local partners through a program website. Partners can access materials directly from the site, including posters for store windows, referral slips, and brochures. Many program websites also provide information about upcoming financial education classes and other events.

*Training*

Training frontline staff in financial institutions and community organizations is an important component of Bank On initiatives. These staff must be well-versed in the program's components since they are usually the first point of contact for potential customers. Some programs use online training tools, presentations and videos to reach a large number of frontline staff at one time. This method is particularly useful for statewide Bank On programs and other initiatives that are spread out over large geographic areas. For instance, Bank On program planners in Louisville, KY and Indiana, as well as in Manhattan regularly host webinar trainings for financial institution and community organization staff about their Bank On programs. Bank On Seattle-King County leaders created a training DVD, which outlined program details and was provided to all participating financial institutions to be shown to their staff. The video was also useful for sharing program information with the public.

*Data Tracking*

Some programs have used technology in creative ways to improve their data tracking efforts. For example, the Los Angeles Community Development Department partnered with community-based organizations to collect a rich set of data from potential and current Bank On customers. With the help of funders and other experts, program staff developed a computer-based intake questionnaire that gathers information about residents' current financial services usage, level of debt, income and perceived future financial services needs. The questionnaire is delivered to clients of partnering community organizations and helps the city track the impact of the program on clients' financial security. In Seattle-King County, Bank On partners developed a simplified online reporting tool to help financial institution staff enter information directly using a shared form that can be submitted on line.

## Bank On Program Impact: Tracking Outcomes

Because the Bank On field is still relatively new, there has been little research or evidence to date that tracks the impact of the model on individuals' financial stability. However, all Bank On programs attempt to track some basic information about whether they are meeting their goals. Most Bank On programs have straightforward goals for opening a certain number of new accounts, typically 10 to 20 percent of the estimated number of unbanked residents in the area served (which has ranged so far from 500 to 200,000 new accounts) over one to two years. Other goals have included decreasing the number of check cashers in the community, increasing access to financial education, increasing the number of people using direct deposit, and concentrating resources and attention toward specific demographic groups such as homeless residents, youth, and seniors.

In general, Bank On initiatives track the following information:

- Basic account information, such as the number of Bank On accounts opened and closed;
- Account performance details, such as the average monthly balance, use of debit cards or other account features, and non-sufficient fund (NSF) occurrences;
- Marketing information that indicates how the customer learned about the program; and
- Indicators demonstrating what knowledge customers retain from financial education and how that education affects their success as accountholders.

These data are tracked by participating financial institutions and reported to program leaders or federal regulators. There have been many challenges associated with the data tracking process. Many initiatives have not collected

Banking on Opportunity
A Scan of the Evolving Field of Bank On Initiatives
US DEPARTMENT OF THE TREASURY 25
Office of Financial Education and Financial Access

additional data on program impact beyond what is listed above because financial institutions do not track individual outcomes and conducting additional research can be cost prohibitive, an issue explored in greater detail below.

Program Outcomes

To date, all initiatives that have collected account data for at least one year have met their initial goals for opening accounts. The table below presents basic account data tracked for a sample of programs (these data include a selection of programs launched between 2006 and 2010): As discussed further under the section, Challenges for Bank On Initiatives – Tracking Data and Assessing Impact, below, aggregating data on accounts opened by individual financial institutions and from individual Bank On initiatives has posed to be a challenge, thus it is not possible to aggregate the numbers from all Bank On sites to date.

Account Results from Selected Bank On Programs

| Program Name | Number of New Accounts Opened | Additional Information |
|---|---|---|
| Bank On Cowlitz County | 1,311 (first 8 quarters) | 821 savings accounts 490 checking accounts |
| Bank On Denver | 1,318 (7 of 10 banks reporting, first quarter) | |
| Bank On Evansville | 1,930 (approx. 8 quarters, data since February 2009) | |
| Bank On Indy | 12,980 (5 quarters) | |
| Bank on Fresno | 51,458 (7 quarters, through October 2010) | |
| Bank On Los Angeles | 56,550 (8 quarters) | |
| Bank On Louisville | 1,712 (2 quarters) | average balance of $970 |
| Bank On Manhattan | 7,200 (first 2 quarters) | |
| Bank On Sacramento | 36,444 (8 quarters) | |
| Bank On San Francisco | 78,000 (approx. 16 quarters) | average balance of $900 |
| Bank On Seattle-King County | 43,000 (approx. 9 quarters) | |
| Bank On St. Pete | 1,785 (5 quarters) | average balance of $246.74 |
| Bank On D.C. | 2,600 (3 quarters) | |
| Bank On California[45] | 214,236 (8 quarters) | |

45 Bank On California results include all of the cities under the Bank On California umbrella, including those which are listed in this table.

26  US DEPARTMENT OF THE TREASURY
Office of Financial Education and Financial Access
Banking on Opportunity
A Scan of the Evolving Field of Bank On Initiatives

Indirect Benefits of Bank On Programs

Bank On programs have had far-reaching outcomes on communities beyond the opening of accounts for underserved families. For some communities, particularly small or rural communities, a Bank On initiative provides a unique opportunity that did not previously exist to bring together important stakeholders around issues concerning financial access. Cities and states are well-positioned to use the coalitions and "infrastructure" developed through Bank On initiatives to initiate other programs that help families build and protect assets. For example, local officials in Gaithersburg, MD were able to use their Bank On program as a launchpad for the development of an outreach campaign connecting residents to free tax preparation services and the federal Earned Income Tax Credit. Since then, Gaithersburg leaders have been encouraging local employers to provide opportunities for their employees to participate in financial education, open accounts, and directly deposit paychecks into their accounts. A Bank On initiative can offer an initial "hook" that draws the attention of local officials to the financial challenges facing low- and moderate-income families.

Another unanticipated benefit of Bank On initiatives is the way in which they enhance community focus on financial education. In many communities, new partnerships with financial education providers are developed through the Bank On initiative, which offer opportunities to coordinate services more effectively for local residents. In Indianapolis, First Lady Winnie Ballard's primary interest is improving financial literacy within her community. The Bank On Indy initiative helped her draw partner organizations' attention to an issue about which she felt strongly.

In Seattle-King County, the Bank On initiative provided the infrastructure to develop a broader financial stability event called "Financial Fitness Day," which was co-sponsored by Bank On Seattle-King County. The event included activities such as free tax preparation, credit report review, screening for public benefits, college financial aid assistance, job search assistance, loan information, financial planning, home buying and mortgage application assistance, starting or growing a small business, avoiding identity theft, and legal assistance on financial issues, as well as opening accounts. The event drew a large audience and enabled recently elected Mayor Mike McGinn to tout the importance of financial access and act as a champion for the event.

## Keys to a Successful Program

Early Involvement of Local Elected Officials and Financial Institutions

Local elected leaders often provide the initial spark for a Bank On campaign. Because local elected officials are usually highly visible, have strong name recognition, and are trusted voices in the community, they are a natural fit as the public face of the initiative. In addition, local officials have the leverage needed to engage a diverse set of stakeholders, especially financial institutions, and create a common, community-wide agenda around which partners can coalesce. Programs that have had little or no elected official involvement have had a more difficult time securing the involvement of financial institution partners and have experienced greater delays in project development.

Bank On initiatives have found that the earlier financial institutions are engaged, the more likely they are to become significantly involved in the initiative. For example, many program leaders have met individually with bank and credit union representatives to secure participation commitments prior to formally announcing the program and creating committee planning structures. Individuals leading a Bank On programs have found it important to engage either high-level financial institution staff who are authorized to make decisions, or representatives who have direct access to those staff. In Evansville, IN, an Old National Bank representative was integral in getting the Bank On initiative off the ground and has since assisted in the development of programs throughout the region served by the bank.[46]

---

46 Old National Bank's footprint includes Indiana, Kentucky, and Illinois.

Early and Thorough Planning

San Francisco's in-depth planning process as well as the experiences of other cities demonstrate that the early stages of a Bank On initiative can have a tremendous impact on the program's long-term success. More than half of Bank On initiatives surveyed by NLC required six to 12 months to plan their initiative prior to launch, which gives an indication of how much time is required to engage stakeholders and conduct thorough planning. Of the different "components" that comprise a Bank On program, many city officials have noted that developing a budget and creating a data tracking plan are perhaps the most important components for early planning.

In launching a Bank On initiative, local entities are faced with the challenge of developing the program without substantial or centralized funding. Developing a budget at an early stage gives stakeholders a figure from which to "work backwards" and identify how to meet specific resource needs. For example, by estimating the cost of marketing and outreach, Bank On Newark leaders were able to tailor their requests for contributions from financial institutions to ensure that they would have enough funds.

Early identification of and agreement on data tracking and analysis can also help mitigate some of the challenges described later in this report. Communities that have given early thought to this component have more success obtaining sufficient data from financial institutions.

Robust Partnerships and Organized Planning Structures

A variety of partners adds depth and provides the resources needed to develop and sustain a Bank On program. Community organizations have direct connections to the target population and provide invaluable assistance in outreach and financial education. Financial institutions develop and deliver the low-cost products. City staff serve as coordinators and conveners. Federal regulators have the capacity to help convene stakeholders and to impartially collect and analyze data from banks and credit unions to determine program impact. Each partner's role has proven to be complementary for creating a successful program, though the structure and composition of the partnerships tend to vary from community to community.

Every Bank On initiative has created some type of steering committee or work group structure to guide planning and implementation. Based on San Francisco's model, most have chosen to create similar planning structures that include an overall steering committee to guide the work, as well as subcommittees that focus on the key components of a successful Bank On campaign. In general, these are: financial products and services; marketing and outreach; financial education/money management; and tracking and evaluation.[47]

Setting Measurable Goals

Setting measurable goals has been an important strategy for ensuring that stakeholders remain engaged around a common agenda and measuring the success of the initiative. Bank On programs typically set goals for number of accounts opened but have also sought to achieve goals such as decreasing the use of alternative financial services or increasing access to financial education. Many of the more mature Bank On initiatives, including those in San Francisco, Fresno, and Savannah, have created annual reports that highlight goals and accomplishments. These documents are particularly effective in showcasing impact and garnering support for Bank On initiatives.

Community Needs Assessments and Preliminary Research

Assessments of the financial services landscape in a community have been valuable for highlighting local needs. These assessments often have a geographic component and identify how many residents lack bank or credit union accounts, barriers to access, and availability of mainstream and alternative financial services by neighborhood.

---

47  National League of Cities, "Bank on Cities: Connecting Residents to the Financial Mainstream."

Many local Bank On program planners have conducted preliminary research. San Francisco leaders received planning assistance from the Brookings Institution. Some communities received assistance from national organizations such as NLC or through the U.S. Department of the Treasury's CFAP. The CFAP community consultants identified potential partners in each of the program's eight sites, as well as challenges and strengths specific to the communities in order to help them convene the most appropriate partners and implement the best approaches. NLC facilitated connections between city programs and organizations providing research assistance. These organizations included the Pew Charitable Trusts, which developed financial access profiles containing a snapshot of a city's unbanked residents and a map of mainstream and alternative financial services, and the William J. Clinton Foundation, which helped cities conduct research on the financial landscape of specific neighborhoods.

Information about the unbanked and the communities' financial landscape helped local stakeholders clearly define needs, leverage support and gain attention to the issue of financial access, create a baseline from which to develop measurable goals, guide program development, engage funders and partners, promote the development of appropriate financial products, and better evaluate the success of the program.

### Flexibility versus Uniform Standards

Bank On initiatives are locally planned and driven. The flexibility inherent in this type of model is an important strength because it allows cities to meet the unique needs of their unbanked residents. For example, Bank On Newark included a low-cost remittance in their standard Bank On product after learning from surveys that many residents needed that option. In Savannah, Bank On leaders engaged the faith-based community because of its high level of trust and influence among residents in the community. Bank On Savannah hosts outreach events at houses of worship and works with religious leaders to distribute outreach materials and information about financial education opportunities to congregations throughout the city.

However, the variation in programs that comes with flexibility can also create tension between local initiatives and national financial institutions that may prefer to offer a basic product across the regions they serve. This tension is further explored in the next section.

## Challenges for Bank On Initiatives

### Tracking Data and Assessing Impact

Tracking and evaluation has been a constant challenge for Bank On programs because financial institutions are often limited in the information they are able and willing to track, and local governments and other partners have no authority to enforce data collection. It is often not feasible to track consumer outcomes beyond the aggregate number of accounts opened and basic account activity, and many financial institutions do not collect additional demographic data. In addition, confidentiality requirements restrict what kind of data financial institutions are able to share with outside partners. For example, financial institutions would be prohibited from releasing individual account details that Bank On program staff may want to compare with other data collected from residents. Because of this lack of individual-level data, it is difficult to understand how Bank On initiatives affect the communities they aim to serve, influence the financial behaviors and choices of those who open an account, and determine why a customer closes an account.

Also, because financial institutions are the point of entry for the Bank On initiative, other partners may have little or no opportunity to interact directly with Bank On clients. This lack of access makes it difficult to connect customers with other beneficial services, such as financial education or credit counseling. Bank On coordinators also cannot follow up to verify whether customers were counted and tracked.

There is not a strong enforcement mechanism to ensure that financial institutions track and report data consistently. Even if a Bank On program requires participating financial institutions to track and report data, program staff find it difficult to obtain accurate and timely information. From the financial institution's perspective, it may not be easy to track these data. Tracking account information is an added responsibility for bank and credit union staff. Financial institutions that are unable to incorporate Bank On accounts into their existing electronic tracking systems effectively may have difficulty presenting accurate information. It may also be difficult to define and flag "Bank On" accounts consistently across financial institutions, and different institutions may be tracking different populations of Bank On customers.

When data are tracked, they are self-reported and not verifiable. There may not be consistent definitions or measures of account activity tracked across all programs. For example, the term "average monthly balance" can mean a different thing to different institutions. Even the definition of "unbanked" can vary across and sometimes within programs. Despite efforts to clarify the process, there is no independent oversight to determine if accounts are accurately tracked. This lack of consistency may lead to both overcounting and undercounting.

Also, because data are tracked on a per account basis, not by individual accountholders, financial institutions track only the number of accounts opened and not the number of individuals banked. For example, one person may open more than one account, or may close one account and open another at a different financial institution and therefore be counted twice. Banks and credit unions have no way of comparing accountholders to see if duplicate accounts are being tracked.

Finally, the rate of staff turnover in financial institution branches can be high and new staff may not have sufficient information about the program or understand their role in directing potential customers to the Bank On product and capturing important data at the point of opening an account

Other Financial Institution Considerations

Local governments and community organizations have had to navigate sometimes uncharted waters when partnering with financial institutions through the Bank On process. This section identifies some of the challenges beyond data tracking that arise from their participation.[48]

First, the support and engagement may vary by financial institutions' size, mission, and the level of commitment of individual financial institution representatives. Financial institutions are concerned with the amount of staff time dedicated to what is often a six to 12-month negotiation process just to launch the program. They may also balk at having staff participate in numerous meetings, especially as they begin to engage in multiple local Bank On programs that may need to be staffed by the same financial institution representative. Some Bank On programs have found it easier to work with credit unions (both CDFI and non-CDFI) because by mission and design, these institutions are more focused on the needs of low or moderate income consumers and members.

Many financial institutions face challenges in training staff about the various elements of the Bank On initiatives, including products, coding of accounts for data collection purposes, and referrals to and from financial education providers. For a financial institution with multiple branches, hundreds of staff members need to be trained regularly, as staff turnover is common in front line positions, such as tellers.

---

48  This section draws on research by CFED exploring financial institutions' experiences with participation in Bank On programs, as well as field research conducted by the National League of Cities over the last three years with Bank On programs and their relationships with financial institution partners.

In addition, financial institutions' flexibility in meeting certain product criteria varies by type of institution. For example, credit unions, community banks and CDFIs may already be offering low-cost products and services to the unbanked market, which may facilitate their participation in a Bank On initiative because they do not have to modify their existing products and policies, and may also be able to respond more easily to program requirements due to having smaller footprints. Larger banks, on the other hand, are more likely to standardize products and services across markets and may therefore be less willing to modify or create a new type of account. The local branch managers of larger banks are also less likely to have the ability to make concessions or change existing policies. For example, the Bank On Newark product includes one free money order per month. At least one larger bank was not able to comply with this requirement and as a result could not be part of the program. Some large bank partners are eager to innovate and to participate meaningfully in the Bank On model, but prefer to do so in a standardized way, which can be frustrating for local initiatives trying to negotiate local features.

Although credit unions and local or regional banks may have more flexibility to modify or create new products for a local market or open accounts for unbanked customers, there is a tradeoff between having more consumer-friendly product standards and engaging a larger number of participating financial institutions, which often serve a larger market share. Larger banks have been important players in Bank On initiatives due to their larger resources, geographic reach and multiple locations. Many larger banks also have appropriate products aimed at the unbanked market segment, but these products are often not well advertised. Moreover, some consumers may be more likely to open an account at a large bank because they recognize the bank's brand.

Smaller financial institutions face their own unique challenges. Because credit unions and community banks generally already offer products that more closely match the needs of the unbanked, Bank On products, which are developed in negotiations that include banks, can sometimes end up being "weaker" or "watered down" by comparison since large banks do not share the same mission as many of the smaller institutions. Moreover, credit unions can feel excluded because of the "Bank On" language.

Nevertheless, credit unions and community banks benefit by being a part of a community-wide initiative that provides opportunities for exposure and for better serving the community. For example, Express Credit Union, a CDFI credit union based in Seattle, benefited from its involvement in Bank On Seattle-King County's financial education network and Financial Fitness days by gaining increased opportunities to build relationships with potential new members. The credit union also appreciates the relationships the initiative fosters among participating financial institutions and the increased customer base gained. For example, other participating credit unions will refer their customers to Express if they cannot serve them.[49]

The negotiation process between coalition partners and financial institutions, regardless of size and type, can be particularly time-consuming, complicated and challenging because of the conflicting interests of these entities. While the Bank On model aims to increase the supply of products that are appropriate for unbanked consumers, financial institutions are also concerned about their profit, risk, and security. Some financial institutions fear that a defined financial product that looks similar across institutions will impact their competitiveness within the market, and want the flexibility to change their products when needed or to express what they feel is their unique brand value proposition. For example, Bank On San Francisco leaders negotiated with financial institutions during a robust economy and created a Bank On product that was financially acceptable at that time. Since that time there has been a significant recession and major upheaval in the financial markets. It is unclear if financial institutions will be willing to offer such products in the future. Research conducted by the Center for Financial Services Innovation (CFSI), seems to support the uncertainty going forward, financial institutions are becoming more conservative, which may result in moving away from unbanked customers, rather than expanding their share of this market.[50]

---

49  Interview with Dave Sieminski, Managing Director of Express Advantage, the non-profit affiliate of Express Credit Union. April 2011.

50  "The Future of Financial Services." 2011. Webinar. Chicago, IL: Center for Financial Services Innovation.
    Available at: http://cfsinnovation.com/content/future-financial-services-1. Hereafter, CFSI 2011 Webinar.

Some additional product challenges include:

- While some initiatives have sought to develop more innovative products, they have found that financial institutions are hesitant to stray from what their peers have already undertaken in other Bank On programs. The product criteria developed by Bank On San Francisco inadvertently became a ceiling, and most subsequent initiatives have struggled to convince financial institutions, especially some of the larger banks, to offer additional features, such as eliminating overdraft protection charges, providing free money orders, capping monthly fees at $5, or removing opening balance requirements.[51]

- Similarly, as more Bank On campaigns emerge, large national banks struggle to respond to multiple requests from different initiatives around the country or a region.

- Financial institutions are concerned with the amount of time dedicated to the product negotiation process. It can also be time consuming to engage financial partners. Communities in which a high-level elected official is not engaged can struggle to reach agreement on product criteria.

- Some financial institutions have concerns about federal regulations pertaining to safety and soundness and customer identification mandates under the Bank Secrecy Act and USA PATRIOT Act. Since lack of acceptable identification is a major barrier to banking, these concerns can impact the reach of a Bank On initiative.

It may be that new types of financial products and services will be effective at meeting the needs of LMI customers in a manner that is sustainable for financial institutions. Such innovations may take the form of prepaid cards, or other services that employ greater use of technology. Innovations may also be built on partnerships among financial institutions, non-profit organizations, employers and others in order to determine and fill the regular financial service needs of consumers in a cost-effective manner.

Funding Limitations

Although Bank On programs cost relatively little, some funding is necessary for conducting an effective marketing campaign, coordinating large numbers of partners and using creative new strategies to improve financial access outcomes. The economic downturn has made it difficult for communities to allocate funding for innovative and comprehensive programs. Bank On initiatives typically rely most heavily on contributions from financial institutions and in-kind resources provided by coalition partners. All of these resources have diminished in the current economic climate.

For some of the larger banks participating in multiple programs, there may be inconsistencies in contribution policies and practices. For example, a bank may contribute a certain amount to one program, but only offer a fraction of that amount to another program. Additionally, some banks may not be comfortable with funding multiple programs across the state or region they cover, or providing significant support over time.

At the same time, community organizations, cities and states have been forced to reduce staff hours, increase other responsibilities, or lay off workers who often provide staff time to coordinate programs because of overall budget cuts. Enhancing the ability to dedicate sufficient staff to program implementation would be a major boost for programs that rely on staff or volunteers from multiple partners.

---

51  "Building Better Bank Ons: Top 10 Lessons From Bank On San Francisco". Phillips, L. and Stuhldreher, A.. February 2011. Available at:  http://newamerica.net/publications/policy/building_better_bank_ons

## Maintaining Momentum

Many initiatives have struggled to keep coalition partners engaged and enthusiastic over time, particularly during long negotiation periods, times when the program development process becomes temporarily stalled, in the face of leadership transitions, or after launch. Planning meetings often require many hours of negotiation that can cause some level of "burnout." Some initiatives have found that partners remain fully engaged until after the launch, at which point their enthusiasm and participation begin to wane. The period following the launch can be a key point at which efforts to maintain enthusiasm of local partners can ensure proper implementation and support any needed mid-course corrections.

## Financial Education Delivery

As described earlier, financial education is a common component of Bank On initiatives. Yet many initiatives struggle with how to successfully deliver financial education so that it is convenient and appropriate for participants and improves their ability to maintain accounts and achieve financial stability. Research shows that the success of financial education programs has been mixed.[52] There has been little quantitative evidence to suggest what specific curricula, formats, or delivery methods have the most impact on LMI individuals in helping gain greater financial stability, and innovation may be needed to enhance the cost-efficiency of financial education efforts. However, many Bank On leaders have reported that some type of financial education or counseling is important to ensure that Bank On participants successfully manage their accounts, and many report that financial education is well received and appreciated by participants.

Financial education is especially a topic of concern for communities that lack existing financial education opportunities. In these communities, locating appropriate, affordable curricula and instructors, as well as training opportunities for those instructors, can be a significant challenge. In some instances, Bank On leaders have chosen to develop their own new financial education component.

Communities with sufficient existing financial education programs face a different challenge related to coordination of services. Bank On program staff may identify a set of criteria or core competencies that can be used to ensure local financial education classes are appropriate for Bank On customers, and cover the content deemed appropriate by the financial institution partners. A second challenge is to coordinate the various classes to ensure that they offered at times and places convenient to the target audience. Child care, transportation and language barriers remain difficult obstacles for families seeking financial education. Bank On programs must consider these challenges when making referrals to financial education providers.

## Changing Regulatory Environment and its Impact on Financial Institutions

The financial services sector has undergone major changes in recent years, causing financial institutions to change their own products and programs. Recent financial regulatory changes may reduce financial institutions' revenue from overdraft charges and interchange fees. According to research conducted by the CFSI, the financial crisis and resulting new regulations are causing financial institutions to be more conservative about their willingness to offer products to higher-risk markets or lower income consumers.[53] These changes can impact Bank On initiatives ass and credit unions reconsider how to offer appropriate products to the unbanked.

---

52 See: Collins, Michael J. 2010. "A Review of Financial Advice Models and the Take-up of Financial Advice." Madison, WI: The Center for Financial Security. Available at: http://cfs.wisc.edu/Publications-Briefs/A_Review_of_Financial_Advice_Models_and_the_Take-up_of_Financial_Advice.pdf; see also: Lyons, A.C., Palmer, L., Jayaratne, K.S.U, and Scherpf. E. 2006. "Are We Making the Grade? A National Overview of Financial Education and Program Evaluation." *Journal of Consumer Affairs*, 40: 208–235..

53 CFSI 2011 Webinar.

- Overdraft fees have traditionally brought in millions of dollars in revenue for financial institutions but have also been highly controversial.[54] A customer who overdraws his or her account on a purchase by just a few dollars could be charged up to $40 in fees. As a result, the Federal Reserve implemented changes to Regulation E, which stated that as of July 1, 2010, financial institutions could not charge overdraft fees for everyday debit card and ATM transactions unless the customer had "opted in" for the service. Financial institutions can no longer automatically include overdraft protection when someone opens an account.[55]

- Interchange fees are the fees that financial institutions receive every time a purchase is made with a debit card. The current fee that financial institutions receive is 1.14 percent of the purchase. The Dodd-Frank Wall Street Reform and Consumer Protection Act of 2010 included an amendment, known as the Durbin Amendment, which directs the Federal Reserve Board to consider limiting the interchange fees that banks can charge, particularly for debit cards. The Federal Reserve Board has established a cap in these fees of approximately 24 cents per transaction.[56] Smaller banks, with assets of less than $10 billion, would be exempt, although they may still be impacted if they use the same card providers.[57] This would reduce fees earned by debit cards by 60-80 percent and is estimated to cost the banking industry between $4 billion and $14 billion per year.[58]

As a result of these two changes, it may become increasingly difficult for Bank On initiatives to negotiate free or low-cost checking accounts. Several banks have already announced increases in their monthly fees for basic checking products, the elimination of certain rewards programs, and additional requirements that clients needs to meet in order to avoid fees. In some cases, the new, higher fees are above the guidelines agreed upon in local Bank On initiatives. These changes also create confusion for Bank On clients who have opened accounts with the assurance of transparent, low costs that would not change. Changing and hidden fees and costs are often the reason that many Bank On customers have either had negative experiences with banks or have avoided opening accounts in the past. There is tension when financial institutions find it necessary to change a product in a way that is contrary to their Bank On product agreement. Bank On initiatives are left with the choice of either renegotiating their product criteria to accommodate the new fee structure or asking those financial institutions to leave the collaborative.

Leadership Transitions

Because Bank On initiatives are often driven by local elected champions, a change in administration can potentially disrupt an initiative. When an elected official leaves office, there is a risk that his or her successor will not continue to support the initiative, particularly if it is an initiative that is closely tied to the preceding administration. Bank On programs that have navigated this transition successfully, including San Francisco, Seattle-King County, and St. Petersburg, have done so because the program has been embedded in the infrastructure of the city and the community and because local leaders have supported maintaining the program. Elected official and staff transitions can be particularly challenging to a program that is still in the planning and has not yet launched the development stages.

54 Paletta, Damian. "Fed Slaps Curbs on Overdraft Fees." November 2009. *The Wall Street Journal*. Available at: http://online.wsj.com/article/SB10001424052748703811604574532063720902686.html; see also: "Quick Facts on Overdraft Loans." 2009. Washington DC: Center for Responsible Lending. Available at: http://www.responsiblelending.org/overdraft-loans/research-analysis/quick-facts-on-overdraft-loans.html.

55 "Highlights of Final Rules Regarding Overdraft Services." November 2009. Washington DC: Federal Reserve Board. Available at: http://federalreserve.gov/newsevents/press/bcreg20091112a2.pdf.

56 Federal Reserve Board Press Release, June 29, 2011. Available at: http://www.federalreserve.gov/newsevents/press/bcreg/20110629a.htm.

57 Summary of the Durbin Amendment on Interchange Fee Reform (Section 1075 of the Dodd-Frank Wall Street Reform and Consumer Protection Act).

58 Interchange Fee Study conducted by Cardhub.com based on data from based on data from The Nilson Report, annual reports from both VISA and MasterCard, and information from VISA and MasterCard's interchange assessments. Updated March 2011. Available at http://education.cardhub.com/interchange-fee-study-2010/.

The Evolving Field of Financial Access

The Center for Financial Services Innovation (CFSI) has identified a number of factors affecting the financial access field in the coming years, presenting both challenges and opportunities for Bank On programs.[59]   First, demographic changes may increase the importance of connecting residents to mainstream financial services.  One challenge involves addressing the needs of an aging population, including many older adults who have experienced increasing debt over time or have few assets as they approach retirement.  In addition, a substantial portion of recent population growth has been driven by the immigration of new residents, who are more likely to be unbanked.  Finally, the youth and young adult population – more adept at using technology products – may be alienated from the traditional financial system and could benefit from some of the newer, innovative technological changes in the financial market.

The economic environment has changed dramatically since the start of the first Bank On initiatives.  As a result, anecdotal evidence indicates that advocates and practitioners are likely to deemphasize the promotion of homeownership as an asset-building strategy and instead shift their focus to workforce development and savings (e.g., for emergencies, education, and retirement). Additionally, as lending standards have tightened, it appears that many underserved individuals will need credit building and repair services as well as access to alternative underwriting of affordable, sustainable mortgages made on reasonable terms.

According to CFSI research, regulatory reforms and technological advances are changing the types of financial products offered by financial institutions as well as the costs of products and services.  As noted above, new regulatory rules could potentially lead financial institutions to become more risk averse.[60]

Demographic and technological changes are also creating incentives for new financial service providers to enter the market.  Over the past several years, large retailers such as Wal-Mart and Kmart have begun offering a range of low-cost financial products.  In addition, a range of non-bank financial service companies such as Mango Financial and Progreso Financiero have created new products, such as prepaid debit cards and web- and mobile-based applications with advertising strategies that market specifically to low-income populations and communities of color, and which may provide terms and pricing that are better than "fringe" providers in the marketplace.  Thus, there may be a new set of reasonable alternatives to both financial instutions and alternative financial service providers. While the goal of the Bank On model is to connect consumers to financial institution accounts, these new products may offer appropriate choices either as "transition" products to mainstream banking, or in some cases, as alternatives.

Gaps within the Financial Access Field

Although a basic transactional bank account can be considered the primary point of entry into the financial mainstream, unbanked and underbanked individuals must have access to a variety of safe, affordable products in order to fully protect and build their assets.  While Bank On and other financial access initiatives have been effective at connecting unbanked residents with basic bank accounts, additional financial products such as small-dollar loans, microenterprise credit, savings options, and niche products like prepaid debit cards can also be valuable components of a broader asset-building strategy.

### Financial Access on the Horizon

In communities around the country, new opportunities to expand financial access beyond transactional accounts have emerged, with cities building broader financial stability initiatives atop their Bank On efforts.  Although collaborations change over time, maintaining a shared objective of helping families become financially stable will

---

59  CFSI 2011 Webinar.

60  CFSI 2011 Webinar.

Banking on Opportunity
A Scan of the Evolving Field of Bank On Initiatives    US DEPARTMENT OF THE TREASURY    35
Office of Financial Education and Financial Access

enable Bank On programs to withstand changes in leadership, maintain focus, and take new steps to improve outcomes for residents. Broad-based financial access initiatives, whether they predate or grow out of Bank On efforts, can help cities make progress toward this goal.

As Bank On leaders assess whether the initiative meets the specific needs of unbanked consumers in their communities, they may consider expanding the program to reach a larger number of residents after the pilot phase or first year, adding new features or services to supplement the baseline product, reaching out more intentionally to certain segments of the population, and connecting the Bank On initiative with other asset-building opportunities.

Integration with Other Financial Services

A Bank On program or other financial access initiative can offer a platform for testing and delivering innovative financial products for underserved populations. Several Bank On programs incorporate other types of financial services into their product suite such as short-term, small-dollar loans, credit-building and repair services, acceptance of alternative data for evaluating credit and making alternative loans, and innovative savings options.

For example, Bank On programs in San Francisco, Savannah, and Seattle-King County have developed a small-dollar loan product or payday lending alternative. In Seattle-King County, three Bank On partners (one bank and two credit unions) are offering loans of up to $1,000 at an 18 percent annual percentage rate. Since San Francisco's Payday Plus program was launched in 2010, six financial institution partners have made 300 Payday Plus loans to customers, with loans capped at $500.

Some communities are encouraging customers to directly deposit their paychecks into bank accounts. City leaders in San Francisco, Savannah, and Gaithersburg work with local employers to encourage, and in some cases mandate, the use of direct deposit. Employers are often willing partners since direct deposit not only helps their unbanked employees save but also lowers their administrative costs.[61]

Some emerging Bank On programs are in the planning stages of considering other ways to promote saving. For example, Bank On Save Up KC!, which encompasses Kansas City and some surrounding towns, is combining its Bank On program with an America Saves campaign. This program will have a greater emphasis on savings than other Bank On initiatives.

Bank On D.C. and Bank On Denver are both considering the development of a business component to their initiatives to ensure that local entrepreneurs and small businesses have access to safe, affordable products that meet their specific business banking needs. Business accounts in traditional banks often charge high fees or are designed for larger companies. Programs are also offering products that in some ways model the convenience of higher-cost fringe services but are more affordable and still meet the needs of unbanked residents. For example, Bank On Central Texas partnered with Mango to offer a prepaid debit card that met the same "low cost" standard as the program's transactional bank account ($10 or less per month).

According to the limited evidence gathered to this point about account openings, Bank On and similar initiatives appear to open new pathways to the financial mainstream for a large segment of the unbanked population. However, several segments of this population face unique barriers to the financial mainstream and often remain underserved. Their diverse financial services needs are not always met by the products available through Bank On and other financial access initiatives.

---

61  Many Bank On programs have formal and informal agreements with their financial institution partners regarding what is expected of them, the baseline product features they are agreeing to, and what type of reporting they expect of them.

Targeting Specific Populations

As Bank On initiatives become established in their communities, they can increasingly target tailored products toward specific segments of the unbanked and underbanked population. For example, a community with a college or university may have a disproportionately large number of young adults who are unbanked or underbanked. A prepaid debit card offered as part of a Bank On initiative's product suite may be appealing to this population and help introduce them to the financial mainstream.

Many programs are interested in targeting vulnerable or underserved neighborhoods. Bank On Indy conducts targeted outreach to residents living in the largest low-income housing complexes in the city's two lowest-income neighborhoods. Some Bank On programs located in areas with large Muslim populations are trying to find ways to make their products comply with Islamic banking rules. Other key constituencies may include people with disabilities, rural residents, or the youth population.

*Financial Access for People with Disabilities*

According to the U.S. Census Bureau, as of 2004, there were approximately 32 million adults (ages 18 or over) with disabilities living in the U.S. Although most research on the unbanked has not specifically focused on people with disabilities, the National Disability Institute estimates that thirty percent of adults with disabilities do not have either a basic checking or savings account, and are much more likely to be asset poor than the general population.[62] Additionally, research on taxpayers with disabilities suggests that they may need to be given special consideration when designing a financial access strategy. Like the unbanked population overall, these individuals are less likely to have attained a college education and more likely to have lower incomes.[63] While it is not clear if low-income people with disabilities are more likely to be unbanked than other low-income Americans, they do report the need for special accommodations in banking activities. Constraints that they face include teller windows that are too high, a lack of accessible online banking for individuals with visual disabilities, and a lack of understanding among bank personnel of how to respond to the needs of customers with disabilities.[64]

Individuals with disabilities may be particularly concerned that keeping money in bank or credit union accounts could cause them to exceed asset tests for government benefits, and thus run the risk of losing their benefits. Bank On St. Petersburg leaders partnered with the National Disabilities Institute to train program partners on meeting the unique needs of people with disabilities, and are also reaching out to that segment of the community. Based on St. Petersburg's model, all programs within Bank On Florida are incorporating these disability-specific components into their work.

*Financial Access in Rural Communities*

The expansion of the Bank On model has not been as widespread in rural communities as it has been in urban areas. Financial access initiatives are concentrated in urban areas, perhaps due to greater demand as well as stronger capacity and civic infrastructure on which to build such initiatives. However, access to the financial mainstream tends to be more limited for residents living in rural areas. Families in rural areas frequently lack access to affordable financial products, financial education and other asset-building supports such as volunteer income tax preparation sites.[65]

---

62  "The Business Case: Why Target People With Disabilities." Washington DC: National Disability Institute. Available at: http://www.realeconomicimpact.org/Asset-Development-Community/The-Business-Case.aspx.

63  "Taxpayers with Disabilities: 2010 Report." September 2010. Washington DC: Internal Revenue Service. Available at: http://www.irs.gov/pub/irs-pdf/p4640.pdf.

64  "Educating Democracy: Tax and Financial Service Needs of Working Americans with Disabilities." 2006. Washington DC: National Disability Institute.

65  See, for example, "Community Financial Access Pilot Report." 2010. Washington DC: United States Department of the Treasury available at: http://www.treasury.gov/resource-center/financial-education/Pages/CFAP.aspx. and "Asset Building Taking Root in Rural Communities" in Banking and Community Perspectives, Federal Reserve Bank of Dallas, Issue 1, 2011 available at http://www.dallasfed.org/ca/bcp/2011/bcp1101.cfm.

Because rural communities generally cover large geographic areas, families may face transportation and other barriers to access when trying to get to brick-and-mortar financial institutions during the business day. The number of bank and credit union branches in rural, low-income communities is limited. In addition, with many rural communities covering multiple municipalities or counties, overlapping jurisdictional boundaries can create challenges to engaging key stakeholders. Some community organizations and financial institutions may only be interested in serving specific areas or simply may not have the capacity to cover larger geographical areas.

*Financial Access for Youth*

While most Bank On programs focus on unbanked and underbanked adults, there are benefits to reaching youth early with messages about the importance of mainstream banking and savings and providing them with bank accounts and opportunities for financial education. Youth often learn about financial practices from their parents and can develop poor financial habits at a young age. Some Bank On programs target young people. For instance, Bank On D.C. offers an account to young people participating in the city's summer youth employment program. In developing this account, the city first determined which financial institution partners already had products that would be appropriate for the youth. Program leaders encourage participating youth to directly deposit their pay into accounts instead of receiving paper checks. Participants also must attend a financial education class and create a profile on the Bank On D.C. online financial education portal.

Similarly, Bank On Jacksonville has reached out to youth through one of its credit union partners, Vystar, which has developed a special account for students. The account allows for smaller deposits and pays a higher interest rate on certificates of deposit (CDs) and other savings products. Vystar also has bank branches in three high schools in the Jacksonville area. Finally, in an effort to provide appropriate financial education to youth, Bank On Fresno conducted a student survey to assess college students' banking practices and knowledge.[66]

Connecting Bank On with other Asset-Building Opportunities

Access to mainstream financial services is one important step towards financial security but is far from being the only challenge facing underserved families. In addition to the strategies outlined above to expand financial access, a few cities are connecting their Bank On programs with other asset-building strategies by:

- Coordinating a Bank On campaign with local outreach on the federal Earned Income Tax Credit (EITC) and volunteer income tax assistance (VITA) sites. These strategies can help Bank On initiatives reach potential new customers, provide unbanked tax filers with quick access to their refunds, and offer alternatives to a costly refund anticipation loans.

- Promoting savings by working with initiatives like America Saves or AutoSave. These programs offer a way to target new customers while encouraging the use of an important asset-building tool.[67] AutoSave is an employer-based savings plan in which a small amount of an employee's wages are automatically diverted from each paycheck into a savings account. San Francisco is participating in the AutoSave pilot project, which was launched last year with one credit union partner. The San Francisco Treasurer's Office enrolled 40 employees in the first six months of the program, and the credit union provides participants with a small, $50 incentive after six months of savings, which has made the program more successful in San Francisco than in some of its peer pilot sites.

---

66  Pierce, Tamyra. California State University Student Survey Data. 2010. Fresno California: United Way of Fresno County and Bank On Fresno.

67  AutoSave is program developed and piloted by the New America Foundation which encourages employee savings by working with employers to divert small payroll deductions into a savings account. More information about AutoSave is available here: www.newamerica.net/publications/policy/autosave_0.

- Using Bank On to share information with the public about homeownership counseling, foreclosure prevention scams, or identity theft. For example, the City of Providence, RI, in conjunction with its Bank On initiative, held a Financial Fitness Fair in early 2011. The fair provided residents with an opportunity to open accounts, receive foreclosure and debt counseling, and apply for microloans. As part of its broader financial empowerment efforts, the city and its Bank On partners also hosted a special event to teach residents how to avoid foreclosure rescue scams.

- Connecting Bank On customers to public benefits and social services or working with social service providers to connect clients to the Bank On program. The Seattle-King County Asset Building Collaborative, which was instrumental in developing Bank On Seattle-King County, created a training for social service providers on financial empowerment principles. This training is intended to prepare case managers with financial knowledge that will help them better serve their clients, who are referred to the Bank On initiative if they do not have an account.

Potential Roles for State and Regional Initiatives

While regional Bank On efforts that are either countywide or involve two or more cities are likely to be similar to a city-led program, statewide initiatives have an opportunity to serve two important roles. First, they can help cultivate new local programs by providing technical assistance, leveraging connections with statewide partners, and assisting local programs in understanding financial regulations. Additionally, they can help leaders of statewide Bank On programs share best practices and resources. It is important that statewide programs clearly define their role and their relationship with existing local Bank On programs.

State-based programs may also be able to overcome financial access challenges facing rural areas and smaller towns, which often lack the resources and infrastructure necessary to get a Bank On effort off the ground. Even if a rural area does not have sufficient resources or lacks the political will to start an initiative, a statewide program can support the development of a Bank On program in a nearby, "anchor" town or city that serves (e.g., through grocery stores or post offices) the wider rural area. Bank On Indiana leverages resources from the statewide partnership of Community Action Agencies, the Indiana Housing and Community Development Authority (IHCDA), and Indiana Bankers Association, the Indiana Credit Union League and other entities to assist smaller communities.

While the Bank On field is still relatively young, there is great potential to build on the successes observed so far at the local level and create a nationwide program that addresses the needs of underserved families and helps them achieve financial stability. With further analysis and careful consideration of the changing financial environment, Bank On programs can be continuously improved to ensure that more families have access to safe, appropriate financial products.

## Appendix 1: Bank On Program Information

| Program Name | Launch Date | Contact Information: Program Lead and Website |
|---|---|---|
| *City Based Programs* | | |
| Central Texas (Austin) | June 2010 | Emily De Maria<br>Vice President, Community Development<br>United Way Capital Area<br>Austin, TX<br>512-225-0366<br>emily.demaria@unitedwaycapitalarea.org<br>www.bankoncentraltexas.org |
| Brazos Valley (Cities of Bryan and College Station, TX) | March 2011 | Ronnie L. Jackson<br>Neighborhood/Youth Services Manager<br>City of Bryan<br>979-209-5115<br>rjackson@bryantx.gov<br>www.bryantx.gov/bankonbrazosvalley |
| Carbondale, IL | April 2010 | City Hall<br>618-457-3226<br>bankoncarbondale@ci.carbondale.il.us<br>ci.carbondale.il.us/index.php?q=bankoncarbondale |
| Dallas, TX | June 2010 | Jerry Allen<br>Councilmember<br>City of Dallas<br>216-670-4068<br>Jerry.allen@dallascityhall.com<br>www.dallascityhall.com/BankOnDallas |
| Denver | October 2010 | Katherine O'Conner<br>Analyst & Bank on Denver Project Manager<br>Office of Economic Development<br>Denver, CO<br>720-913-1528<br>katherine.oconnor@denvergov.org<br>www.bankondenver.org |
| Detroit, MI | March 2011 | Derrick Headd<br>Fiscal Analysis Division<br>Detroit City Council<br>Detroit, MI<br>313-224-4524<br>headdd@detroitmi.gov<br>www.bankondetroit.org (note, this website will not be live until late April) |

| | | |
|---|---|---|
| Evansville | February 2009 | Patty Avery<br>Assistant Vice President & Community Outreach Officer<br>Old National Bank<br>812-465-8802<br>patty.avery@oldnational.com<br>bankonevansville.org |
| Fresno, CA | December 2008 | Sevag Tateosian<br>Manager, Financial Stability Services<br>United Way of Fresno<br>Fresno, CA<br>559-243-3664<br>stateosian@unitedwayfresno.org<br>www.bankonfresno.ca.gov |
| Gaithersburg, MD | September 2009 | Cindy Hines<br>Olde Towne Revitalization Coordinator<br>Department of Economic Development, City Manager's Office<br>Gaithersburg, MD<br>301-258-6310 x2107<br>chines@gaithersburgmd.gov<br>www.gaithersburgmd.gov/poi/default.asp?POI_ID=1764&TOC=107;81;87;1764 |
| Greenfield, IN | 2010 | Larry McGuire<br>lmcguire@greenfieldin.org<br>Their website is listed as: www.greenfield.org, but it is currently down |
| Houston, TX | May 2008 | Shannon Dionne Nobles<br>Deputy Director<br>City of Houston Controller's Office<br>832-393-3403<br>shannan.nobles@houstontx.gov<br>houstontx.gov/bankonhouston/index.html |
| The Heartland (Omaha) | March 2011 | Julie Kalkowski<br>Financial Hope Collaborative<br>Creighton University<br>402-280-3792<br>juliekalkowski@creighton.edu<br>Website still under development |

Banking on Opportunity
A Scan of the Evolving Field of Bank On Initiatives    US DEPARTMENT OF THE TREASURY   41
Office of Financial Education and Financial Access

| | | |
|---|---|---|
| Indianapolis, IN | October 2009 | Natalie R. Clayton<br>Deputy Director<br>Greater Indianapolis Progress Committee<br>Indianapolis, IN<br>(317) 327-3625<br>nclayton@indy.gov<br>bankonindy.org |
| Jacksonville, FL | October 2010 | Karen Landry<br>Executive Director<br>War on Poverty - Florida, Inc.<br>904-766-7275<br>klandry@waronpoverty.org<br>www.bankonjacksonville.com/about/ |
| Kalamazoo, MI | April 2010 | Jeffrey H Brown<br>Executive Director<br>Poverty Reduction Initiative<br>Kalamazoo, MI<br>269-387-2678<br>director@haltpoverty.org<br>www.haltpoverty.org/bank_on_initiative |
| Kansas City, MO | June 2011 | Kevin W. Shields<br>Community Affairs Specialist<br>Federal Deposit Insurance Corporation<br>(816) 234-8158<br>Kshields@fdic.gov<br>www.bankonsaveupkc.org |
| Los Angeles, CA | March 2009 | Abigail R. Marquez<br>Senior Program Manager<br>Community Development Department<br>Los Angeles, CA<br>213-744-9307<br>abigail.marquez@lacity.org<br>www.bankonla.org/index.htm |
| Louisville, KY | July 2010 | Tina Lentz<br>Executive Administrator<br>Louisville Metro Human Services<br>502-574-6827<br>tina.lentz@louisvilleky.gov<br>www.louisvilleky.gov/economicdevelopment/<br>BankOnLouisville |

| | | |
|---|---|---|
| Madisonville, KY | February 2011 | Leslie Curneal<br>Executive Assistant to Mayor<br>Madisonville, KY<br>270-824-2100<br>lcurneal@madisonvillegov.com<br><br>Kent Mills<br>Old National Bank<br>Kent.Mills@oldnational.com<br>www.bankonmadisonville.com/partners.html |
| Manhattan | July 2010 | Shira J. Gans<br>Policy Analyst<br>Office of the Manhattan Borough President Scott Stringer<br>New York, NY<br>212-669-2206<br>sgans@manhattanbp.org<br>bankonmanhattan.com |
| Memphis, TN | March 2011 | Kerry J. Hayes<br>City of Memphis<br>kerry.hayes@memphistn.gov<br>901-576-6017<br><br>Charles "Corky" Neale<br>Director of Research<br>Rise Memphis<br>corky@risememphis.org<br>bankonmemphis.org |
| Muncie, IN | February 2011 | Gary Chenault<br>President<br>United Way of Delaware County<br>Muncie, IN<br>gchenault@uwdcin.org<br>765-288-5586 ext. 230<br>www.invitedtoliveunited.org/index/bankonmuncie.asp |

| | | |
|---|---|---|
| Newark, NJ | November 2009 | Frank Martinez<br>Policy Advisor<br>Economic and Housing Development Department<br>Newark, NJ<br>373-733-8413<br>martinezf@ci.newark.nj.us<br><br>Anthony Santiago<br>Chief Operating Officer<br>Newark Now<br>973-733-3460<br>anthony@newarknow.org<br>bankonnewark.org |
| Oakland, CA | April 2009 | Tyrone Cosey<br>Operation HOPE<br>510-535-6700<br>Tyrone.cosey@operationhope.org<br>bankonoakland.ca.gov |
| Owensboro, KY | April 2010 | Keith Sanders<br>The Lawrence & Augusta Hager Educational Foundation<br>270-685-1603<br>ksanders@lahef.org<br>www.owensboro.org/node/402 |
| Philadelphia, PA | October 2008 | Brian Dries<br>Office of the Controller<br>City of Philadelphia<br>215-686-8869<br>brian.dries@phila.gov<br>philadelphiacontroller.org/bop |
| Providence, RI | April 2010 | Garry Bliss<br>Bank on Providence Coordinator<br>Department of Planning & Development<br>Providence, RI<br>401-339-4681<br>gbliss@providenceri.com<br><br>bankonprovidence.org |
| Sacramento, CA | January 2010 | Kimberlie Gladden<br>City of Sacramento<br>Kgladden@cityofsacramento.org<br><br>Russell Fehr<br>City of Sacramento<br>Rfehr@cityofsacramento.org<br>www.bankonsacramento.ca.gov |

| | | |
|---|---|---|
| San Francisco, CA | September 2006 | Leigh Phillips<br>Program Manager<br>Office of the Treasurer and Tax Collector, Office of Financial Empowerment<br>City and County of San Francisco<br>415-554-4479<br>leigh.phillips@sfgov.org<br>bankonsf.org |
| San Jose, CA | December 2008 | Jim Dale<br>United Way Silicon Valley<br>408-345-4347<br>Jim.dale@uwsv.org<br>bankonsj.org |
| Santa Ana, CA | September 2009 | Natalie Bishop<br>Orange County United Way<br>949-660-7600<br>NatalieB@UnitedWayOC.org<br>www.bankonsantaana.ca.gov |
| Savannah, GA | March 2009 | Robyn Wainner<br>Asset Building & Financial Services Manager<br>Step Up Savannah<br>912-232-6747<br>rwainner@stepupsavannah.org<br>stepupsavannah.org/bankonsavannah |
| Seattle-King County, WA | September 2008 | Jerry DeGrieck<br>Public Health Manager and Policy Advisor<br>Seattle Human Services Department<br>Seattle, WA<br>206-684-0684<br>jerry.degrieck@seattle.gov<br>everyoneiswelcome.org |
| St. Petersburg, FL | August 2009 | Gary Jones<br>Planning & Economic Development Department<br>City of St. Petersburg, FL<br>727.893.7877<br>gary.jones@stpete.org<br>bankonstpete.org |

| | | |
|---|---|---|
| Tippecanoe (Lafayette, IN) | March 2011 | Robert D. Smith<br>Market President<br>Old National Bank<br>Lafayette, Indiana<br>765-420-8664<br><br>Marie Morse<br>Executive Director<br>Homestead Consulting Services<br>Lafayette, In<br>765-423-1284<br>Marie@homesteadconsulting.net<br>www.bankontippecanoe.org |
| Washington, DC | May 2010 | Sybongile Cook, Project Manager<br>Office of the Deputy Mayor for Planning &<br>Economic Development<br>202-285-4845<br>sybongile.cook@dc.gov<br>www.bankondc.org |
| *State Based Programs* | | |
| Bank On California | December 2008 | Bev Augustine<br>Department of Consumer Affairs<br>916-574-8203<br>Bev.augustine@dca.ca.gov<br>www.BankonCalifornia.ca.gov |
| Bank On Florida | December 2010 | Bill Mills<br>407-797-6549<br>Director of Strategic Initiatives<br>Florida Prosperity Partnership<br>bill.mills@bankonfl.org<br>www.floridaprosperitypartnership.org/bank_on_<br>program0.aspx |
| Bank On Indiana | October 2009 | Christopher Conner<br>Treasurer of State's Office<br>317-232-6387<br>cconner@tos.in.gov<br><br>Patty Avery<br>Old National Bank<br>812-465-7278<br>Patty.Avery@oldnational.com<br>www.bankonindiana.com/ |

| Bank On Illinois | October 2009 | Primary contact in transition www.bankonillinois.org |
|---|---|---|
| *County Based Programs* | | |
| Bank On Cowlitz County, WA | February 2008 | Liz M. Myntti Financial Independence Center Program Manager Certified Educator in Personal Finance Lower Columbia CAP 360-425-3430 x 215 LizM@LowerColumbiaCAP.ORG www.cowlitzsaves.com |
| Bank On Marion County, FL | 2010 | Maureen Quinlan President United Way of Marion County, Inc. 352-732-9696 mquinlan@uwmc.org www.uwmc.org/our-work/financial-stability/bank-on-marion |
| Knox County, IN | June 2010 | United Way of Knox County and City of Vincennes Amanda Quirk 812-882-3624 knox@unitedwayofknoxcounty.org www.bankonknoxcounty.com |

## Appendix 2: Bank On Case Studies Overview: Savannah, GA and Seattle-King County, WA

This report provides an in-depth picture of two sites – Seattle-King County, W.A. and Savannah, GA– that have developed initiatives designed to promote access to mainstream financial banking and financial education as a way to enhance the overall financial stability of their residents. Both cities have implemented a "Bank On" initiative, modeled after the Bank On San Francisco program.

### The Bank On Model

The Bank On model, first developed in 2006 by the City and County of San Francisco, is driven by partnerships. Local leaders, community organizations, financial institutions, and other community stakeholders work together to create financial access pathways for un- and under-banked individuals to connect to safe, affordable financial services. Bank On programs aim to increase the supply of "starter account products" by developing baseline product criteria that participating financial institutions agree to offer, informing unbanked consumers about the benefits of account ownership and encouraging them to open accounts, and raising community wide awareness of the issue and risks associated with being unbanked. Related goals of decreasing the reliance on check cashers, payday lenders, and other predatory financial services and making quality money management education more easily available to underserved populations have also been very important. Shortly after Bank On San Francisco's launch, efforts to replicate the model have grown across the country.

### Seattle and Savannah: Early Pioneers

Seattle-King County and Savannah were among the small handful of communities that began efforts to replicate the Bank On model almost immediately after San Francisco's launch. Both cities took part in a site visit conducted by the National League of Cities to San Francisco to learn about the model in August of 2006, just before San Francisco's program launched. Following this visit, city leaders from both cities began the challenging work of bringing together key stakeholders with the purpose of launching similar programs. After over a year of strategic planning, Seattle was the second city in the nation to implement a Bank On program. The City of Seattle and the Seattle-King County Asset Building Collaborative brought together a wide range of financial institution partners, community partners, and public agencies to develop the initiative and ensure its success through extensive outreach across King County.

Savannah followed Seattle-King County in April 2009 with the launch of Bank On Savannah as a means to address the large number of unbanked households throughout the city and to serve as a tool for reducing poverty and promoting economic development. Step Up Savannah, the city's anti-poverty collaborative organization, has served as the overall coordinator for the Bank On Savannah program. Step Up actively links Bank On with other asset-building efforts throughout the community, such as financial education.

As of June 2011, both Seattle-King County and Savannah maintain successful Bank On initiatives that have met their initial program goals, and continue to expand and innovate. During its first two years, Bank on Seattle-King County has documented the opening of over 54,000 new accounts for previously unbanked customers with an average balance of $652 in checking accounts and $932 in savings accounts. In Savannah, a much smaller city, 1,011 Bank On accounts were opened, the majority (86 percent) of which remained open after one year.

Both communities have faced similar challenges in program implementation related to data collection and reporting, training of financial institution staff, and financial sustainability. However, both programs have also experienced similar successes as a result of having committed city leadership and strong partnerships with financial institutions and community organizations.

About the Case Studies

These two case studies were developed by the National League of Cities through a contract with the U.S. Department of Treasury to provide an in-depth view of the development and implementation of Bank On programs, including an analysis of the challenges and successes they face. Seattle-King county and Savannah were selected from a small group of cities that have had Bank On programs in operation for at least a year. Cities were selected by representatives from the National League of Cities, CFED, the New America Foundation, and the City of San Francisco. Savannah and Seattle were chosen from this group based on the following criteria: city size, demographic diversity, time length of program operation , and unique program features.

The case studies were authored by consultants working for the National League of Cities based in Seattle and Savannah, and then further reviewed and edited by the National League of Cities. The Seattle case study was authored by Diana Stone, Director of Initiatives, Seattle-King County Asset-Building Collaborative and the Savannah case study was authored by Andrea Silverman, Independent Consultant. Information was collected from interviews with key program leaders in each city including city government representatives, financial institution partners, community organizations, and Bank On customers.

## Appendix 3: Bank On Savannah Case Study

Executive Summary

In spite of a growing economy in the City of Savannah, GA, 22.8 percent of the city's residents live in poverty, and an estimated one in eight of the city's 52,000 households is unbanked. In April 2009, Bank On Savannah was launched to address the number of unbanked households throughout the city and to serve as a tool for reducing poverty and promoting economic development. Step Up Savannah, the city's anti-poverty collaborative organization, serves as the overall coordinator for the Bank On Savannah initiative and grant-financed financial education programs. Step Up actively links Bank On with other asset-building efforts throughout the community.

City leaders first became interested in the idea of connecting residents to the financial mainstream in 2006 after they learned it through the National League of Cities' (NLC) Helping Families Build Assets technical assistance project, where they were exposed to the Bank On model. Convinced that this model of reaching financially underserved residents with mainstream banking products could play a significant role in helping Savannah residents move out of poverty, city leaders began the process of developing their own Bank On initiative. With strong support from Mayor Otis Johnson and a robust infrastructure of asset-building and poverty reduction work, Savannah was well-positioned to implement a successful Bank On initiative. In December 2006, Step Up Savannah (Step Up) helped to convene a Banking Task Force that spent the next two years developing Bank On Savannah.

The Banking Task Force consisted of representatives from seven banks, the City of Savannah's Economic Development Department, the Chatham Savannah Asset Development Coalition, and Step Up. Working in smaller committees focused on product development, marketing and data tracking and evaluation, the Banking Task Force developed a Bank On initiative based on local and national research on the needs of the unbanked, as well as the resources available in the community; this includes strong community-based organization involvement, robust financial education offerings, and leadership from financial institutions.

In 2009, Mayor Otis Johnson formally launched Bank On Savannah. The first year was a success with 1,011 Bank On accounts opened, the majority (86 percent) of which remained open after one year. Other positive impacts that were seen included over 3,000 financial education clients served and five major employers increased their direct deposit take-up. The program has also faced some challenges in its implementation phase, including reaching and engaging the targeted population and ensuring consistent, accurate data collection from financial institutions.

Bank On Savannah Product

The financial product criteria developed is designed to meet the specific needs of unbanked residents in Savannah. After a strategic negotiation process, the members of the Banking Task Force developed the following product criteria:
- Waiver of first NSF (insufficient funds)/overdraft fee
- Opening deposit requirement under $100
- No monthly minimum balance
- No (or low) monthly fee
- ATM and debit card access
- Promotion of linked savings account
- Direct deposit
- Free online banking
- Refer customers to financial education
- Accept Mexican Matricula Consular card as primary identification and accept an individual Taxpayer Identification Number (ITIN) in lieu of social security number

- Open accounts for people on ChexSystems if the activity is more than six months old, except in cases of fraud, or where bank requirements for restitution not met
- Open accounts for people with low or negative credit scores (bank discretion).
- Review Bank On Savannah checklist at account opening with customer to inform them of parameters and responsibilities

## Bank On Savannah: Looking Ahead

In its relatively short existence, Bank On Savannah has met its initial goals and succeeded in bringing mainstream banking services and financial education to many unbanked residents of the city. The program development process also had an added benefit of developing strong between the city and financial institutions. There were several factors that contributed to the success of the program. Some of these include building a foundation for the program through preliminary research on the community's needs, strong support from the mayor and other city leaders, an engaged banking community, and access to the lessons learned from other cities that had already developed similar initiatives.

Mayor Johnson continues to be a strong champion of the Bank On program. Moving forward, Bank On Savannah plans to expand outreach efforts-- focusing on the city's Hispanic population-- and increase training for financial institution staff, including efforts focused on improving data collection. The initiative also hopes to introduce more products, such as small dollar credit builder loans, and to bring back an alternative refund anticipation loan program (ARAL) that had ended in 2010.

## Background and History

Savannah is a historic, coastal Georgia city with population of 136,000. The downtown area, which includes 22 squares and centuries old architecture, has been declared a National Historic Landmark district. In addition to having a very strong tourism industry, Savannah has the fourth largest container port facility in the U.S., is a regional center for medicine and higher education, and has aerospace and other manufacturing industries. Savannah is located within Chatham County which includes seven other municipalities: Bloomingdale, Garden City, Pooler, Port Wentworth, Thunderbolt, Tybee Island and Vernonburg. The country is served by eighteen commercial banks with a total of 97 offices and total deposits of $4.6 billion.[68]

In spite of its growing economy, 22.8 percent of Savannah's residents live in poverty, and an estimated one in eight of Savannah's 52,000 households is unbanked.[69] The Bank On Savannah, formally launched by Mayor Otis Johnson in April 2009, was to address this deficit and serve as a tool for reducing poverty and promoting economic development.

The roots of the Bank On Savannah program go back to the 1990s, when the city's traditional efforts to improve neighborhoods through investment in "bricks and mortar" were expanded to include a broader program of actions to achieve poverty reduction. Bank On Savannah eventually grew out of this large scale effort to reduce poverty within the city. Following the election of Mayor Johnson in 2004, the City joined with Chatham County, representatives of several private sector and community organizations, and the University of Georgia to conduct research on poverty and develop a Poverty Reduction Action Plan. That plan, published in 2005, describes a large number of barriers to poverty reduction, including the limited access of low-income residents to mainstream financial institutions. The plan identifies five broad, strategic areas of action: asset-building, workforce development, housing, dependent care, and health. To facilitate and coordinate the implementation of the Action

68  Information about banks from the Federal Deposit Insurance Corporation (FDIC) website: www.fdic.gov.

69  "FDIC National Survey of Unbanked and Under-banked Households. 2009. Washington DC: Federal Deposit Insurance Commission. Available at: http://www.fdic.gov/householdsurvey/.

Banking on Opportunity
A Scan of the Evolving Field of Bank On Initiatives
US DEPARTMENT OF THE TREASURY
Office of Financial Education and Financial Access
51

Plan, an executive director was hired using city resources, and the organization, called Step Up Savannah, was born. Step Up Savannah, which was the organization that was the driver behind the City's Bank On efforts, is a collaborative of organizations with a unique leadership structure. The quasi-governmental organization is supported by the city government but relies on a collaboration of organizations and volunteers to accomplish its goals. The collaboration includes businesses, community organizations and government agencies, all with a mission of reducing poverty in Savannah and Chatham County by helping families move toward economic self-sufficiency. Step Up accomplishes this goal through three primary focuses: workforce development and jobs; wealth building and financial understanding; and work supports.

Step Up's board of directors is comprised of community and organizational leaders from city and county government, local business, educational institutions, nonprofit organizations, and low-income neighborhoods. Step Up's executive director, Daniel Dodd, explains that Step Up has purposely remained small as an organization. Rather than implementing programs, Step Up acts primarily as a convener and collaborator, bringing groups together and working with them to find innovative solutions.

The City's Poverty Reduction Action Plan called for action teams to be formed to address each strategic area outlined in the plan. Each team is chaired by volunteers who are members of Savannah's private, local government and nonprofit sectors. The City's financial access efforts grew out of the work of one of these teams – the Banking Task Force. In 2011, six years after the inauguration of Step Up, the following teams have been established:
- Banking Task Force
- Workforce Action Team
- Employer Supports Action Team
- Chatham County Safety Net Planning Council
- Financial Education Network
- Residents Team of Neighborhood Leaders
- Chatham Savannah Asset Development Coalition (which existed prior to the formation of Step-Up but became linked with Step Up as one of the action teams)

Each of these action teams is led by volunteers from partnering organizations and supported by Step Up staff.

### Evolution of the Savannah Banking Task Force

The Banking Task Force emerged in 2006 after growing interest from city leaders in the idea of promoting financial access for Savannah residents. A year earlier, in 2005, Savannah was one of eight cities selected to join the National League of Cities' (NLC) Helping Families Build Assets Technical Assistance project. The objective of the two year project was to build municipal leaders' capacity to take action toward helping families increase their economic stability. In June 2006, the final project meeting was held in San Francisco with a focus on showcasing the newly developed Bank On San Francisco program. Savannah City Manager Michael Brown, Step Up Director Daniel Dodd, and the Asset Development Coalition Chair Edward Chisolm returned from San Francisco convinced that Savannah needed to expand its asset building activities and initiate a program to give Savannah's unbanked population access to mainstream financial services. They realized that for it to succeed, the participation and leadership of the banking community itself was essential. Shortly after returning to Savannah, City Manager Brown called the City Executive of Savannah's BB&T Bank, Toby Moreau, and asked him to take leadership of a Banking Task Force which could serve to identify the needs of underserved residents and deliver safe products and services to meet those needs.

The first meeting of the Banking Task Force took place at the BB&T Bank in December 2006, and was attended by representatives from seven banks, the City of Savannah's Economic Development Department, the Asset Development Coalition, and Step Up. At first, Banking Task Force members struggled with how best to achieve the goal of banking the unbanked, and progress seemed, at times, very slow. Much of the discussion focused on how to bring back old customers who were listed on ChexSystems, which involved requiring those customers to make at least partial restitution for earlier debts to the banks and to attend financial education training.[70] Under Moreau's leadership, the number of Banking Task Force participants grew to 10 banks – four community banks and six regional or national banks.

During the task force's formative years, the banks worked to define the common characteristics of the accounts to be offered at each bank (see Box 2). Later, with the assistance of the FDIC, a generic checklist was created to assist bank personnel in reviewing the Bank On Savannah account with new customers. One of the banks, Carver State Bank, already had such an account available, a "Second Chance" checking account. The other three community banks adopted their own versions of what later became labeled a "Bank On Savannah" account. The six regional and national banks used products created by their corporate headquarters, but agreed to follow Bank On guidelines, including the addition of the following criteria that had not been a part of their original second chance products:

Box 1

> ## Bank On Savannah Participating Financial Institutions
>
> - BB&T Bank
> - Capitol City Bank & Trust Company
> - Carver State Bank
> - First Chatham Bank
> - Sea Island Bank
> - SunTrust Bank
> - The Coastal Bank
> - The Savannah Bank
> - United Community Bank
> - Wells Fargo Bank

1. waiver of first NSF (non-sufficient fund)/overdraft fee;

2. referral of customers to financial education; and

3. consideration to opening accounts for people on ChexSystems or with low or negative credit scores.

In practice, the differing standards among the 10 banks led to occasional referrals between banks so that a customer rejected at one bank might be given an account at a second bank.

---

70 ChexSystems is a national database for banks that provides information based on check verifications and consumer credit about a potential customer's banking history and is primarily used to identify people who have had past problems with accounts. Most financial institutions havepolicies against opening accounts for individuals placed on this list.

Box 2

---

### Characteristics of a Bank On Savannah Account

- Waiver of first NSF (insufficient funds)/overdraft fee
- Opening deposit requirement under $100
- No monthly minimum balance
- No (or low) monthly fee
- ATM and debit card access
- Promotion of linked savings account
- Direct deposit
- Free online banking
- Refer customers to financial education
- Accept Mexican Matricula Consular card as primary ID and accept an ITIN in lieu of social security number
- Open accounts for people on ChexSystems if the activity is more than 6 months old, except in cases of fraud, or where bank requirements for restitution not met
- Open accounts for people with low or negative credit scores (bank discretion).
- Review Bank On Savannah checklist at account opening with customer to inform them of parameters and responsibilities

---

Bank on Savannah Program Development

In 2008, significant progress was made in the development of a Bank On initiative. Five positive developments helped Step Up and the Banking Task Force to work through the negotiation process eventually leading to the the formal launch of the Bank On Savannah program in April 2009:
- linking of banks with the target underserved population through the Volunteer Income Tax Assistance (VITA) sites;
- successful design and then piloting (in early 2009) of an alternative financial product, the Alternative Refund Anticipation Loan (ARAL);
- completion of the Neighborhood Financial Services Study financed by the William J. Clinton Foundation;
- expansion of Savannah's financial education programs through a grant from the AIG Financial Literacy Fund; and
- the involvement of representatives of the FDIC and the Federal Reserve Bank of Atlanta in Savannah's initiative.

*Linking of banks to the VITA sites*

In January 2008, the Asset Development Coalition chair invited the members of the Banking Task Force to send bank staff to its VITA sites to assist clients in establishing bank accounts to receive income tax refunds, including earned income tax credits (EITC), by direct deposit. As explained by Teinique Gadson, coordinator of the VITA sites, "we wanted the VITA clients not only to open accounts to get their direct deposits, but also to establish a relationship with mainstream banking." Their experience was that "by having the banks at the VITA sites they are able to touch on other banking issues in a setting in which people felt comfortable asking questions." Gadson discovered numerous instances of "cross-selling," where in addition to opening bank accounts, individuals learned about and accessed lower cost auto loans and credit cards through their discussion with bank and credit union representatives at the VITA sites. This was an unexpected benefit of the effort.

*Piloting of Alternative Refund Anticipation Loans (ARALs)*

For years, commercial income tax preparation businesses in Savannah had been offering Refund Anticipation Loans (RALs) to their clients, charging them an average of $450 in interest and fees plus the income tax preparation fee to allow them to immediately access their expected refunds. City leaders in Savannah saw many residents spending large sums of money at these establishments and wanted to offer an alternative that could help residents obtain their refund through a safe, quick, and affordable loan product. Using a similar program in San Antonio as a model, Banking Task Force members developed the ARAL or Alternative Refund Anticipation Loan at an inexpensive rate. In January 2009, it was offered at two VITA sites through Georgia's Own Credit Union. The ARAL was a successful product and was expanded in 2010. Unfortunately, the program could not be offered in 2011 as a result of an Internal Revenue Service policy change that limited information available to tax preparers.[71]

*Neighborhood Financial Services Study*

To support the work of the Banking Task Force and the development of a Bank On Savannah program, Step Up sought the assistance of the William J. Clinton Foundation to conduct a Financial Services Study focused on Savannah's poorest neighborhoods. The survey was administered by Professor Deden Rukmana of Savannah State University, with the assistance of students and community leaders. It surveyed a randomly selected sample of 201 of the 2,813 households living in Savannah's six poorest census tracts, all located near downtown Savannah.[72] Of those households, 38 percent had neither savings nor checking accounts.[73] Nearly half of the heads of households had never had a bank account at any point in their lives. A majority of both the banked and the unbanked

Box 3

---

### Views of the Unbanked Individuals in Savannah Regarding Mainstream Financial Services (Banks)

As reported in the 2008 study, unbanked respondents indicated that they did not use banking services because:
- fees are too high;
- needing instant access to money and banks take too long to process;
- the government or creditor could take money out of their account;
- they lacked of proper identification required by the banks;
- bank hours were inconvenient;
- they do not have enough money to open an account;
- it is too diffic ult to withdraw money when needed; and
- unwillingness to provide personal information to the bank.

---

Savannah Neighborhood Financial Services Survey, Final Report, 2008.

---

households in those low income neighborhoods routinely used check cashers and money orders, and 11 percent of the sample made regular (weekly or monthly) use of high cost title pawn or title loans.[74] Through the survey, it became clear that (i) there was indeed a very significant number of unbanked residents in Savannah; (ii) both banked and unbanked low-income families depended on high-cost, fringe financial institutions; and (iii) the reasons people did not seek bank accounts were varied and included a distrust of banks, fear of "hidden" fees, and a lack of experience and comfort with banks in general.

71  Starting in the 2011 tax season, the Internal Revenue Service began to remove the debt indicator from its communication process to tax preparers. Before then, both volunteer and paid preparers would receive communication from the IRS after e-filing a person's tax return that would indicate whether or not the taxpayer had a debt that would garnish their federal tax refund. This indicator allowed financial institutions that partnered with preparers to offer RAL and ARAL products to be assured that the loans they were distributing would be quickly repaid through deposited refunds.

72  Census tracts 1, 12, 13, 18, 19, and 101.01, each of which had a poverty rate of > 50% in 2000. Each of these tracts were in Chatham County, GA, Census locator code 130051.

73  Rukmana, Deden, principal investigator, Savannah Neighborhood Financial Services Survey, Final Report, 2008.

74  Savannah has 13 title pawn or title loan businesses, with 29 locations in Chatham County in total.

Banking on Opportunity
A Scan of the Evolving Field of Bank On Initiatives            US DEPARTMENT OF THE TREASURY            55
Office of Financial Education and Financial Access

At the end of 2008 and in early 2009, the study's results were presented and discussed in a series of workshops with the participation of the Banking Task Force members, other community, government and business leaders, as well as representatives of the FDIC, the Federal Reserve Bank of Atlanta, the Clinton Foundation and the Pew Charitable Trust.

*Financial Education Programs*

In early 2008, the Cities for Financial Empowerment (CFE) coalition was created, including Savannah and five other, larger cities. Savannah was able to benefit from the coalition's efforts to secure funding to enhance financial empowerment efforts in participating cities. CFE launched an initiative to expand delivery and increase quality of financial education and counseling services with funding from the AIG Financial Literacy Fund. Funding from the AIG grant helped to finance a full-time Outreach and Financial Education Coordinator, who would be located at the Consumer Credit Counseling Service (CCCS) of Savannah.

The Outreach and Financial Education Coordinator went on to organize the Financial Education Network, a network of financial education providers located within the city. The Coordinator also worked closely with Step Up and the Banking Task Force to ensure that financial education services were offered through the Bank On program . AIG funds were also combined with other existing funds to create another new position at Step Up Savannah which could focus on asset building and financial empowerment activities.

CCCS expanded its financial education program, providing financial education at Savannah's Centers for Working Families and at Savannah's Live Oak Public Library. A financial education directory was developed, as were brochures and a video for marketing the Bank On Savannah and financial education programs. Financial education workshops were also provided at business sites, targeting the employees of Chatham County, the City of Savannah, the Chatham-Savannah Metropolitan Police, the Westin Hotel, and other public and private employers. This effort was aided by the Supporting Work project, financed by the Ford Foundation and implemented by Step Up Savannah.

*Involvement of FDIC and the Federal Reserve Bank of Atlanta*

Two key financial institution regulators, the FDIC and the Federal Reserve Bank of Atlanta, became active in the Savannah Bank On effort toward the end of 2008 when representatives from their Atlanta offices attended a presentation of the results of the Financial Services study.    In spite of the 250 mile distance between Atlanta and Savannah, the FDIC representative became a regular participant in the Banking Task Force meetings, and encouraged Bank On Savannah efforts by offering support and guidance. The FDIC and the Federal Reserve Bank of Atlanta have also contributed to Bank On Savannah by printing materials, producing an informational video about Bank On for Savannah residents, and hosting Bank On committee and other meetings.

Bank On Savannah Launch

After a couple of years of planning, negotiation, and developing partnerships, Bank On Savannah was ready to formally launch. The workshops to discuss the findings of the Financial Services Survey provided both the impetus and the opportunity to take the next step and formally launch Bank On Savannah. The findings from the survey confirmed the challenges that underserved Savannah residents faced when seeking financial services. The presence of external supporters including the FDIC, the Federal Reserve and the Clinton Foundation at those meetings emphasized the importance of the effort. The official launch took place in one of Savannah's historic squares, presided over by Mayor Otis Johnson and the Chair of the Banking Task Force. The ten participating bank representatives each signed a Bank On Savannah "Commitment to Participate," an expression of intent of the financial institution to participate in five key ways:

  (i)     to contribute financial resources to support the effort (expected contribution $750 to $5,000)[75];
  (ii)    to offer the financial products and services that meet or exceed the agreed upon criteria;

75 This financial support was in addition to the in-kind staff support offered by banks to help develop the program.

(iii)    to share data and participate in the tracking of program outcomes;

(iv)    to assist with Bank On Savannah marketing and education initiatives; and

(v)    to attend meetings to assess and improve the effectiveness of the overall campaign.

Beginning with the formal launch, the Banking Task Force set annual targets for Bank On Savannah and has reported annually on its progress. The achievements of Bank On Savannah in its first year, 2009-2010, are presented in Table 1, as are the targets that were set for 2010-2011.

Ongoing Implementation of Bank On Savannah

Following the program launch, the Banking Task Force – now led by Jenny Gentry, market president for Well Fargo in Savannah – has continued to meet every two months. Other active members include representatives of the City of Savannah's Economic Development Department, CCCS, and the Asset Development Coalition. The Banking Task Force has three committees that meet on an intermittent schedule that focus on marketing, data and products. The marketing committee developed and maintains the Bank On Savannah marketing campaign, which is paid for by annual financial institution contributions.

| Bank On Savannah 2009 – 2010 Achievements | Bank On Savannah 2010-2011 Goals |
|---|---|
| • Bank accounts opened –1,011<br>• Accounts still open after one year – 86%<br>• Alternative Refund Advance Loan – 155<br>• Financial Education Clients 3,024<br>• Participating Financial Institutions – 10 banks; 1 credit union<br>• Participating Branch/office locations – 28<br>• 2010 contribution by Financial Institutions to Bank On Savannah -- $15,000<br>• Use of direct deposit increased in 5 large employers | • Bank accounts to be opened –1,500<br>• Accounts still open after one year – 70%<br>• If possible, bring back the Alternative Refund Anticipation Loan – (not offered in 2010-2011)<br>• Financial Education Clients – 3,000<br>• Participating Financial Institutions – 10 banks; 1 credit union<br>• Participating Branch/office locations – 31<br>• Outreach program to Hispanic population developed<br>• Employers' direct deposit programs expanded |

The *marketing* committee has thus far conducted outreach using radio spots, newspaper ads, city bus ads, and the distribution of informational materials and leaflets through community organizations. The use of formal advertising methods has brought the campaign to the attention of news media and the general public. However, committee members indicate they believe that the distribution of Bank On Savannah information through organizations with direct contact with the target population has been the most successful in bringing about greater participation. As a new initiative, the committee is working on approaches to reach the Hispanic population.

The *product* committee's initial work focused on establishing an agreed set of criteria for all Bank On Savannah accounts among the participating banks. It is now examining the impact of financial sector reforms on the program and is also exploring opportunities to expand the Bank On Savannah offerings to include alternative financial products that most meet the needs of financially undeserved residents. The committee is currently concerned with how to re-initiate the ARAL program, and how to provide Bank On customers with access to to credit-building small loans.

The *data* committee has been meeting regularly to address challenges encountered in collecting data on new and existing Bank On Savannah accounts from the 10 member banks. They have worked to streamline the data reporting sheet, gain agreement among the banks on data to be reported, and also regularly follow-up with participating banks to ensure that information is being reportedly quarterly.

Banking on Opportunity
A Scan of the Evolving Field of Bank On Initiatives    US DEPARTMENT OF THE TREASURY    57
Office of Financial Education and Financial Access

Links with other programs

The Bank On Savannah program is linked to several other efforts in Savannah, primarily through the three community-based nonprofit organizations that are active members in the Banking Task Force.

*Step Up Savannah:* In addition to being the overall coordinator for the Bank On Savannah program and grant-funded financial education programs, Step Up actively links Bank On with its other efforts. Step Up works with CCCS to bring financial education and counseling services to Savannah's five Centers for Working Families, to the large organizations involved in its employer program (originally financed by the Ford Foundation), and to the participants of its job training and apprenticeship program for Chatham County. Influenced by the early work of the Banking Task Force, Step Up's employer program actively promotes the use of direct deposit and access to VITA services for low income workers. With the completion of the AIG funded financial education program in 2010, Step Up applied for and received a grant for $150,000 from the Financial Industry Regulatory Authority (FINRA) Investor Financial Foundation. This grant provides financing to Step Up and CCCS to continue to provide financial education and counseling at employer sites, at the Centers for Working Families, and at the Live Oak Public Library.

*Consumer Credit Counseling Service of Savannah:* CCCS is the largest, nonprofit provider of financial education and counseling services in coastal Georgia. As described above, through Bank On, CCCS has expanded its public outreach and education work, and actively promotes the Bank On Savannah program with a wide range of clients.

*Asset Development Coalition:* The chair of the Coalition, who is also the director of Savannah's Neighborhood Improvement Association, a community development corporation that acts as the lead agency for the Asset Development Coalition, continues to invite bank staff to the VITA sites each tax season to help provide access to mainstream financial services for the approximately 5,000 clients of the 12 Chatham County VITA sites. The Coalition is hopeful that the VITA sites will be able to resume offering ARALs in the near future.

Challenges

Savannah had the benefit of strong support for the Bank On program from its Mayor and City Manager, the opportunity to learn from and work with other cities through the NLC and CFE efforts, and financial support from foundations for its financial education programs and research. Nevertheless there were four substantial challenges stakeholders faced in the development and implementation of the program:

1. Reaching the target population. The Banking Task Force realized that for the program to be successful, outreach to the target population was essential. Practical approaches to reaching the target populations through existing community programs and organizations developed slowly, and required new linkages be established between the banks and credit union and community organizations. After some time, these outreach efforts have become successful but require sustained effort maintain its achievements

2. Orientation and training of bank staff. While the initial commitment of 10 of Savannah's banks came relatively rapidly, the necessary orientation and training of the branch managers and frontline bank staff in the participating branches has been a challenge. Given the high turn-over and movement of bank staff, it has been difficult for Bank On leaders to arrange enough frequent trainings and orientations to ensure staff are well-equipped to promote the program and connect customers up Bank On accounts. .

3. Data tracking and reporting. In each participating Bank On Savannah bank, data are collected and reported quarterly regarding the number of new accounts and the status of existing Bank On accounts. However, this has been a significant challenge. For some of the smaller banks, tracking systems can be altered to collect and report new data as required by the Bank On program. However in some of the larger banks, data must be collected manually, as there is no way of tagging the Bank On accounts in most of the banks. As a result,

data are not regularly reported across participating banks. Step Up staff have worked to solicit feedback from banks as to how to improve data collection and have been told that the manual data entry is a challenge. One financial institution representative reported that they would regularly collect and report the data if there were a federal regulation requiring them to do so.

In addition, the definition of what constitutes a Bank On account can sometimes vary between banks. In some cases a Bank On account is only tagged if a customer specifically requests it by name. In other banks, anyone who does not have a bank account is considered a Bank On customer.

4.  Financial Sustainability. Obtaining financial support from banks has been a continuing challenge for Bank On Savannah. In the first year the banks contributed funds for marketing without a great deal of resistance. However, following the financial crisis and gulatory reforms, the initiative is concerned that financial support may be more difficult to obtain in the coming years. In addition, being a smaller city, there are fewer resources from which to draw to build a financially sustainable initiative over time.

## Lessons and Innovations from Savannah

The factors contributing to the success of the Bank On Savannah program include the following:

-   Financial services research. Local data on the numbers of unbanked and the use of fringe financial institutions in Savannah has been invaluable. The dissemination of this research has sparked the interest of many and created support for the Bank On Savannah program.

-   Support from city leadership. In Savannah's case, both the Mayor and City Manager are strong advocates for the initiative. They have used their influence to help the initiative develop, and the Mayor has served as an active spokesperson for the effort. The city has provided funding for key components, including operating resources for Step Up Savannah and funding for the work of the Chatham Savannah Asset Development Coalition.

-   Leadership and teamwork by the banking community. From the beginning, the Bank On Savannah effort has been led by the Banking Task Force, chaired first by the city executive of BB&T and later by the market president in Savannah for Wells Fargo. In addition, involved bankers noted that the success of the program has been aided by their working as a team, an experience that has been personally and professionally rewarding.

-   Role of community-based nonprofit organizations. Step Up Savannah played a central role in supporting the work of the Banking Task Force and in ensuring that community organizations working with low income residents and workers were linked to the efforts of mainstream financial institutions. As stated by Penny King of the Atlanta FDIC, the Bank On Savannah program has benefited tremendously by having "a community-based organization to get marketing to the low and middle income population."

-   Support from key, external organizations. The involvement of external resources, including the FDIC, Federal Reserve Bank of Atlanta, Pew Charitable Trusts, and the NLC put a spotlight on the Savannah effort, provided valuable insights, and lent confidence to the implementers that they were on the right track.

-   Access to program learnings and materials from other cities. Savannah had the opportunity to participate in the NLC asset building technical assistance programs (2005-2008) as well as seminars and workshops organized by the CFE coalition starting in 2008. Both of these city networking organizations provided opportunities for learning from peers that enriched Savannah's initiative. In addition, Bank On materials used in other cities were made freely available to Savannah, reducing its start-up time and costs.

-   Funding for financial education programs and marketing. Access to quality financial education and counseling has been an important component to the program's success. In Savannah, a strong nonprofit organization,

Consumer Credit Counseling Services, led the financial education effort and obtained the necessary funding to do so. Although there have not been any formal evaluations to assess the success of the financial education program to Bank On Savannah's success, anecdotal evidence suggests that customers that go through financial education classes are able to successfully maintain bank accounts.

Future vision

The Banking Task Force continues to provide the overall guidance for the Bank On Savannah program, with the active support of Step Up Savannah. Moving forward, the Bank On Savannah program has several goals which are focused on improving access and quality of services and products for underserved Savannah residents.

*Increase outreach to the Hispanic community.* In 2009, an FDIC survey confirmed the Savannah financial services study findings, and provided new data regarding Hispanic households.[76] The survey found 45.1 percent of Hispanic households in Georgia were unbanked. The findings of this study pointed to the importance of broadening the outreach and marketing of the Bank On Savannah program to include Savannah's Hispanic population. As a result, the Task Force plans to substantially increase outreach to the Hispanic/Latino community, and has a plan for doing so by working with Hispanic churches, community groups and nonprofit organizations.

*Training of financial institution staff and improvement of data collection.* Step Up Savannah's Director of Asset Building and Financial Empowerment has formalized plans to increase the amount and intensity of training for financial institution staff as a way to improve both implementation of the program and data collection.

*Researching impact of lending by fringe financial institutions.* Step Up Savannah has been asked by the Mayor and City Council to research the extent and impact of lending by fringe financial institutions, including Savannah's car title lenders. This is an ambitious project, and the results will provide the Banking Task Force the data it needs to explore issues related to these institutions.

*Development of alternative financial products.* Some members of the Banking Task Force are interested in expanding the availability of alternate financial products such as ARAL's and small credit-builder loans for low income households. Bank On Savannah and the Banking Taskforce will provide the venue for financial institutions and other partners to work towards establishing these product offerings, which will likely be limited to specific banks and credit unions in the initial phases.

---

76 FDIC, 2009

## Appendix 4: Funding and In-Kind Support

| Year | Funding Amount and Source | Nature of Assistance | Specific Use of Funds |
|------|---------------------------|----------------------|-----------------------|
| 2005–2006 | National League of Cities' (NLC) Helping Families Build Assets Technical Assistance project, Phase I | Site visits to cities with advanced strategies in place in financial education, homeownership initiatives, & other asset building programs | Technical assistance only |
| 2006–2008 | NLC Cities Helping Families Build Assets Technical Assistance project, Phase II | Technical assistance from NLC staff and other experts in range of asset building programs | Technical assistance only |
| 2007–2010 | $250,000 Families and Work Institute/Ford Foundation | Supporting Work Project (connecting low income workers with government provided support programs) | Estimated $10,000 used for increasing Direct Deposit and Financial Education at employers' sites. |
| 2008 | $15,000 William J. Clinton Foundation, Clinton Economic Opportunity Initiative | Financial Services Study | Costs associated with study |
| 2008–2010 (2 years) | $200,000 AIG Financial Literacy Fund (component of $1.45 million grant to CFE) | Financial education & counseling | $50,000 per year directly linked with Bank on Savannah activities including marketing, personnel, and financial education. |
| 2011–2013 (2 years) | $150,000 Financial Industry Regulatory Authority (FINRA) Investor Financial Foundation | Financial education & counseling | $35,000 per year used for financial education classes linked with Bank on Savannah. |
| Annual, beginning 2009 | $15,000/year Bank on Savannah Sponsorship by Savannah banks | General funds for Step Up Savannah's support to Bank on Savannah | Administration and Marketing |
| Ongoing, beginning 2009 | FDIC In kind support for printing of brochures and filing of Bank on Savannah video—estimated value of $30,000 | Direct support of Bank On Savannah | Printing of Bank on Savannah materials and development of video |
|  | In-Kind materials | Materials for Bank On Savannah | Bank On materials developed in other cities (San Francisco and others) |
| Annual | $200,000/year City of Savannah $20,000 per year support Bank on Savannah. | Support for Step Up Savannah, general operating costs |  |
| Annual | $110,000/year  City of Savannah This is leveraged by linking all VITA sites with Bank On Savannah | Support for the Chatham Savannah Asset Development Coalition (VITA sites) |  |

## Appendix 5:  Personal Stories of Bank On Customers

Bank On Savannah client – Ms. Erika Wiggins

Ms. Erika Wiggins, a 34 year old working mother of four children, decided in 2008 that she needed to get her financial life together. She was tired of paying exorbitant fees to check cashers and get money orders. She went to Carver State Bank (CSB), a bank that participated in the Banker's Task Force, and asked to reestablish her bank account which had been closed many years earlier due to repeated overdrafts. She was surprised and happy to find that in spite of her low credit rating and negative history with the bank, she would be offered a second chance through CSB's Second Chance Checking program. This program followed the model that was developed by Savannah's Banking Task Force in 2007. The Second Chance Checking account she was given was not substantially different from the other low cost checking accounts offered by CSB. What was different was the level of supervision of the account within the bank and the financial counseling provided to her. The CSB representative talked with Ms. Wiggins about how to manage her account and avoid overdraft problems, quizzed her on her financial goals, and referred her to a Saturday First-Time Homebuyers Seminar. The class was a turning point for her. For years she had worked two jobs – but had never saved a dime. She realized that if she was ever to achieve her goal of buying a home she needed to live on a budget, repay debts, repair her credit, and begin to save. Through Bank On Savannah, she learned about the free tax preparation services offered by the Neighborhood Improvement Association, and began saving the tax preparation fees she had been charged each year. In 2010, she applied for and received CSB's Credit Rebuilder loan for $1,000 and enrolled in a compulsory savings program. Today, in 2011, she is well on the road toward financial health.

62    **US DEPARTMENT OF THE TREASURY**
Office of Financial Education and Financial Access    Banking on Opportunity
A Scan of the Evolving Field of Bank On Initiatives

## Appendix 6: Selected Financial Institution Descriptions

Three Bank On Savannah Banks:Carver State Bank, Coastal Bank and Wells Fargo Bank

**Carver State Bank** (CSB) is a Savannah-based community bank with deposits of $35 million. It is a certified Community Development Financial Institution and is one of only 33 banks in the U.S. that is African American-owned. When the Banking Task Force was formed in 2006, CSB was already providing Second Chance checking, Credit Rebuilder loans, and financial education for its clients. Mr. Robert James, CEO of CSB, has been a major supporter of Bank on Savannah, saying: "The Bank on Savannah Program is part of the asset building approach to get people out of poverty. There is no way out of poverty if you are using check cashers and not involved in mainstream banking." After the establishment of bank accounts, he views credit rebuilding and other ways to bring people into the financial mainstream as "a natural next step" that Bank on Savannah should take to achieve its goals. CSB's Credit Rebuilder loans are short-term (3 year), small size loans (current minimum is $1,500) which require the customer to make regular deposits into savings as well as repaying the loan. The challenge in managing this program is that because of the small size of the loans, the cost in staff time to process the loans is not fully covered by the fees. While the program does not contribute to the Bank's financial bottom line, this and other efforts have earned CSB an "outstanding" CRA (Community Reinvestment Act) rating from the FDIC for the past 6 years.

**Coastal Bank** is a Savannah-based community bank with deposits of $317 million. With the onset of Bank on Savannah, the leadership at Coastal decided that attracting and providing banking services to low income, "high risk" clients was one way the bank could give back to the community. Starting in 2009, Coastal Bank began offering a "Bank on Savannah" free basic checking account targeted to consumers who have little or no banking history. By earmarking the Bank on Savannah accounts, Coastal executives are able to review the status of these accounts and work with customers if they get into trouble. In addition to the somewhat lower minimum balance, the major difference of a Bank on Savannah account from its normal starter checking account is that the bank will accept customers with negative credit and financial histories and in turn will monitor and provide assistance to those customers who are having difficulties. Customers are encouraged to attend financial education sessions, and to use the services of the Consumer Credit Counseling Service if needed. In future, Coastal plans to have a new banking product that makes it hard to overdraw and incur fees. It is also exploring how the new mobile and web-based banking tools may be used by their Bank On customers to manage their accounts and budgets.

With **Wells Fargo's** acquisition of Wachovia Bank in 2010 it established local operations in Savannah with deposits of $969 million. Wachovia was one of the 8 original members of Bank on Savannah. Ms. Jenny Gentry, Market President for Wells Fargo, Savannah, became the chair of the Banking Task Force in 2010. She reports that from the beginning, "the Mayor's initiative on poverty reduction sparked my interest in participating in the Banking Task Force." For Wells Fargo, the development of banking products and services for customers targeted by Bank on Savannah had to result from decisions made at a corporate rather than local level. Wells Fargo met this challenge by creating the "Wells Fargo Opportunity Checking account," a package of services designed to help customers get back into a checking account. Gentry found the 2008 financial services study done in Savannah to be extremely helpful. It showed that while the unbanked do include individuals with negative financial institution histories, many of the unbanked are individuals who have never had a bank account. Wells Fargo has targeted five of its branches for the implementation of the Bank on Savannah program, focusing on branches most accessible to low income households.

Banking on Opportunity
A Scan of the Evolving Field of Bank On Initiatives          **US DEPARTMENT OF THE TREASURY**   63
Office of Financial Education and Financial Access

## Appendix 7: Bank on Seattle-King County Case Study

### Executive Summary

Bank on Seattle-King County (Bank on S-KC) publicly launched in September 2008 with a mission to connect low-income residents to affordable checking and savings accounts and high-quality financial education. The City of Seattle and the Seattle-King County Asset Building Collaborative brought together a wide range of financial institutions, community organizations, and public agencies to develop the initiative and ensure its success. Inspired by Bank on San Francisco, Bank on S-KC established a similar model which includes partnering with financial institutions to provide access to free or low-cost bank and credit union accounts that have a low opening deposit requirements and no monthly minimum balance. The initiative offers a pathway to mainstream financial services for people who previously had trouble managing their accounts, who need to use an alternative method of identification, or anyone else who does not feel comfortable with mainstream banking. Now in its third year, Bank on S-KC can offer the Bank On field some lessons in implementing a successful initiative:

- Integration of financial education: Bank on S-KC partners recognized the importance of financial knowledge and skills for newly banked customers to be able to successfully utilize their checking and savings accounts. They created a network of financial education providers that offered free, high quality financial education to underserved communities. It made the delivery of financial education more accessible, efficient, and effective by avoiding duplication of efforts, sharing resources and information, establishing quality standards, and jointly promoting financial education training opportunities. Furthermore, community organizations and financial institutions have confidence in the quality of the education, enabling them to make referrals or offer incentives for people interested in improving their financial capability.

- Centrality of community partners: With the joint leadership efforts of the Seattle-King County Asset Building Collaborative and the City of Seattle, Bank on S-KC is able to draw on an extensive group of community-based organizations that endorse the initiative as credible and trustworthy to the targeted populations, particularly immigrant and refugee communities. A dedicated Outreach Coordinator provides opportunities to foster direct relationships between financial partners and community groups and can adapt the initiative to changing demographics and needs within the unbanked community. Bank on S-KC is one of many asset-building strategies that partners use to help move struggling families out of poverty and toward self-sufficiency.

- Resources from financial partners: Contributions to the operational costs of the initiative by the financial partners allow the program to hire staff to promote and run the initiative, as well as engage in a substantial public awareness campaigns. Without requiring formal MOUs, financial assessments ensure the necessary commitment to program rules.

- Innovative, well-designed, and functional website: Designed for both unbanked customers as well as social service agency staff, the website includes customized tools to locate appropriate financial institutions and financial education providers for each individual. The website is used to ensure the transparency across products offered by different financial institutions, thus encouraging them to offer accounts with features exceeding the minimum criteria.

Bank on S-KC has also faced challenges. Similar to many other Bank On campaigns, one of the most significant ongoing difficulties is the inability or unwillingness of some participating financial institutions to report all of the agreed-upon data. Because of the existing account-tracking systems, especially in larger institutions, some institutions were not able to "flag" and follow Bank on S-KC accounts. Consequently, the collected data is not complete, which has made an insightful analysis of the program difficult. Bank on S-KC has taken steps to streamline its data collection, and developed an online tool for reporting that should increase the reliability of the data.

Another challenge has been to ensure that all participating financial institution personnel know about the program and the specific products and features offered by their own institution. With over 400 branches throughout the county, some frontline staff are unaware of the details of their own Bank on S-KC product. Greater public awareness and increased training of staff are still required to achieve the goal of welcoming all unbanked customers.

Overall, the financial institution and community partners agree that the Bank on S-KC has provided Seattle's unbanked residents an unprecedented opportunity to access mainstream financial services and high quality financial education. Despite data reporting limitations, the initiative can still be considered a success in its documented opening of over 54,000 new accounts for previously unbanked customers since launching in 2008.

In addition, some financial partners showed flexibility in offering new products, and all agreed that the connections with community partners helped them reach a population that they had not previously served. Community partners welcomed the opportunity to offer clients a safe place for their money and a chance to save and build assets.

## Background and History

Bank on Seattle-King County (Bank on S-KC) was the second Bank On program to launch in the U.S. Inspired by the success of Bank on San Francisco, the idea was proposed in February 2007 by Jerry DeGrieck, Public Health Manager and Policy Advisor in the City of Seattle's Human Services Department (HSD), and Seattle City Councilmember Sally Clark. Working with the Mayor's office, DeGrieck proposed that the City of Seattle take the lead in bringing together the public and private partners that would be required for a successful initiative— government agencies, financial institutions, and community partners.

HSD had received a National League of Cities Institute for Youth, Education and Families' Technical Assistance grant in 2005 to explore how the City of Seattle could improve its asset-building strategies as a method of poverty reduction. Subsequently, the City formed the Seattle-King County Asset Building Collaborative (SKC ABC). The mission of SKC ABC is to create a cohesive and comprehensive system of high-quality, accessible financial empowerment services and networks throughout King County that connects people to mainstream financial services such as financial planning, education, coaching, credit and debt counseling, access to public benefits, free tax preparation, and homeownership and foreclosure prevention resources. SKC ABC was an ideal vehicle to take the lead in moving forward and implementing Bank on S-KC.

This was a key moment to implement such an initiative. Payday lenders in Washington State often charged up to 390 percent APR on loans, stripping residents of hard-earned income. In a 2005 report, the Brookings Institution identified 55 payday lenders and 32 non-bank check cashers in Seattle, charging fees that cost borrowers a total of $15 million dollars and $1.8 million, respectively. In addition, the Washington State Budget and Policy Center found in their analysis "High Interest, Lost Opportunity," that payday lenders, check cashers, and pawn shops are densely concentrated in lower-income neighborhoods. In Washington State, there were 26 such businesses per 100,000 people in the lowest-income neighborhoods (median income below $39,452), as compared to two such businesses per 100,000 people in high-income neighborhoods (median income above $70,887).

The goal of Bank on S-KC is to ensure that affordable financial products are available to everyone. In an effort to assess the magnitude of this challenge, Matt Fellowes with the Brookings Institution estimated in 2005 that Seattle had between 22,745 and 39,215 unbanked households, and roughly 58,349 to 125,675 unbanked adults. Since research shows that twice as many people of color are unbanked as whites, the primary targets of the initiative would be Seattle and King County's significant immigrant and refugee population.

The City of Seattle already had in place a number of initiatives that provided outreach and services to low-income populations, including a public benefits screening tool known as "PeoplePoint," family centers, and neighborhood services centers. The Bank On initiative would support the Human Services Department in achieving its Strategic Investment Plan by helping "vulnerable persons achieve social and economic success." In addition, SKC ABC – with its wide network of community groups that focused their efforts on financial empowerment – was able to provide the leadership and outreach necessary to implement the Bank On campaign.

The City of Seattle and SKC ABC expected financial institutions to be reasonably receptive to developing a Bank on S-KC initiative. Seattle and King County have a high density of mainstream financial institutions throughout most neighborhoods. In fact, the Brookings study found that Seattle's higher-income neighborhoods actually had fewer banks than low-income areas of the city. Bank of America, U.S. Bank, Washington Mutual, and Wells Fargo – four banks already participating in Bank on San Francisco – comprised about 78 percent of the market share in Seattle, which made the idea of engaging financial institutions very realistic. To further bolster the effort, national foundations and think tanks such as the Brooking Institution, the Clinton Foundation and the National League of Cities began paying extra attention to Bank on S-KC in early 2007, and provided it with extra resources and expertise, such as by connecting the program efforts with their own researchers and by offering financial support to bring the Bank on San Francisco team to Seattle in order to act as advisors to the project.

## Development of Bank on Seattle-King County

Under the auspices of the SKC ABC, the City convened representatives from the Federal Reserve Bank of San Francisco, Washington Mutual Bank, the Washington Department of Financial Institutions (DFI), and numerous community and non-profit partners such as United Way, Solid Ground, and Columbia Legal Services to form a working group to address the needs of the unbanked. The City also reached out to Bank on San Francisco representatives and other national partners, such as the National League of Cities, for their guidance.

After several months of initial meetings, the working group settled on a purpose and scope for the initiative:

*People in Seattle and King County who are unbanked will be connected with mainstream financial services including affordable checking, savings, credit, and financial education opportunities. We want to provide people with alternatives to paying exorbitant fees and interest for financial services. The initiative will help people keep more of what they earn and start on a pathway to improved financial success.*

Two significant aspects of this mission expanded upon the Bank on San Francisco model and the City's initial proposal: 1) Financial education became an integral component of the initiative, equal in importance to connecting people with accounts; and 2) the campaign took a county-wide approach due to the integration of the City and County populations and dispersion of low-income people in the area (not just concentrated in City neighborhoods). Financial institutions supported this plan because they had branches throughout the County, many located in lower-income neighborhoods outside the City of Seattle.

With the support and political clout of Mayor Nickels and Councilmember Clark, the working group issued an invitation to all banks and credit unions that had branches located within King County to join the Bank On initiative. The Federal Reserve Bank of San Francisco and the DFI were instrumental in providing names, addresses, and contact information for these financial institutions, and the Federal Reserve sponsored a luncheon during an all-day work session.  In January 2008, an invitation from several key stakeholders, including Mayor Nickels, Councilmember Clark, the Director of the DFI, and the Senior Vice President and Seattle Branch Manager of the Federal Reserve Bank of San Francisco, was sent to all of the financial institutions (Appendecies 10 and 11). The invitation explained the purpose of the "unbanked" initiative and  requested the financial institutions to join a day-long working session to learn more about the proposal and to discuss next steps.  San Francisco City Treasurer José Cisneros and the Bank on San Francisco team, as well as some of their financial institutions and community partners, participated in the meeting and described their efforts, successes, and lessons learned.  Their presentation and convincing data were crucial in demonstrating the feasibility and necessity of the program, and provided guidance to move forward. National League of Cities staff were also present to talk about Seattle's work in a national context.

The work session attracted more than 100 people, representing 35 banks and credit unions and dozens of community partners from SKC ABC.  Interested participants were invited to work together to develop and market financial products and services. Led by the City and SKC ABC, five work groups were formed:

1)  Products and Services
2)  Marketing and Outreach
3)  Evaluation and Tracking of Data
4)  Financial Education
5)  Training of Branch Personnel

Volunteers from the work session began meeting regularly in these groups throughout the next few months. The City and SKC ABC provided direction and staffing, including detailed follow-up notes and draft proposals. Each work group was chaired by a representative of either a financial institution or a community organization. Each group's recommendations were arrived at through consensus and were then vetted to the larger group.  Five initial sponsors for the initiative emerged:[77]

- City of Seattle
- Seattle-King County Asset Building Collaborative (SKC ABC)
- Federal Reserve Bank on San Francisco
- Washington State Department of Financial Institutions
- The Seattle Foundation

The sponsors eventually came to play different roles for the initiative, including lending credibility to the effort (Federal Reserve Bank), acting as the fiscal sponsor (Seattle Foundation), and acting as the data repository (the State Department of Financial Institutions). These roles will be explained in greater detail throughout the report.

By the end of May 2008, the contours of the initiative began taking shape, and financial institutions were asked to commit to the plan. By July, there was consensus on all of the essential elements of the initiative. Similar to Bank

Box 1

> ### Participating Financial Institutions: 2008-2010*
>
> - Bank of America
> - Banner Bank
> - BECU
> - Cathay Bank
> - City Bank
> - Columbia Bank
> - Express Credit Union
> - Frontier Bank
> - HomeStreet Bank
> - KeyBank
> - Pacific International Bank
> - Plaza Bank
> - Seattle Metropolitan Credit Union (SMCU)
> - Seattle Savings Bank
> - United Commercial Bank
> - U.S. Bank
> - Verity Credit Union
> - Viking Bank
> - Washington Mutual
> - Watermark Credit Union
> - Wells Fargo Bank
> - Woodstone Credit Union
>
> *For 2011-2012, City Bank, Pacific International, SMCU, Viking, Watermark, and Woodstone are no longer participating. Following takeovers, mergers, and other corporate changes, Frontier was replaced by Union Bank; Washington Mutual by Chase; United Commercial Bank by EastWest Bank.

77  FDIC and King County were later added as sponsors.

Banking on Opportunity
A Scan of the Evolving Field of Bank On Initiatives          US DEPARTMENT OF THE TREASURY    67
Office of Financial Education and Financial Access

on San Francisco, Bank on S-KC did not require a formal agreement to be signed by the financial institutions, in the fear that developing and signing an agreement would forestall implementing the initiative for many months. Eventually, 22 financial institutions signed on to participate in an initial phase that would last from the fourth quarter of 2008 through the end of 2010.

Program Description

*Products and Services Work Group*

The Products and Services Work Group focused on how to provide affordable, accessible accounts to unbanked people, while ensuring the sustainability of the initiative by making the products reasonably profitable for the financial institutions. The City and SKC ABC used Bank on San Francisco criteria as a starting point for negotiation, since those criteria had already been agreed to by many of the same institutions, but also encouraged the work group to consider pushing the vision furtherby using San Francisco's template as a floor.

A representative from HomeStreet Bank skillfully guided this diverse group, which included large and small bank and credit union representatives, non-profit partners, and one formerly unbanked community member. By providing a forum for all interested parties to express their preferences and develop the criteria, Bank on S-KC ensured the buy-in of participants. The final criteria included the provisions described below.

Each of these criteria represents some amount of compromise. The goal was to encourage as many financial institutions to participate as possible. Program planners recognized that a single institution would be unable to

Box 2

---

### Characteristics of a Bank on S-KC Account

- Minimum opening deposit of $50 or less (Exceptions up to $100 will be noted)
- No minimum monthly balance requirement (beyond what credit unions require for continued membership)
- No monthly service/maintenance fee (Exceptions up to $6/month will be noted)
- ATM or debit cards when accounts are first opened with no fees for own or network ATMs (Exceptions for waiting up to six months to offer an ATM or debit card will be noted).
- One set (one day) of NSF/OD fees waived per year per customer
- Each institution will specify one or more actions they will take in addition to waiving one set of NSF/OD fees, including but not limited to:
  - Savings account or equity line linked to checking account for OD protection
  - Quick communication with customer at time of NSF/ OD (i.e., text messaging)
  - Ability to access account balance immediately
  - Offer account with no OD possibility
  - Offer checkless accounts with ATM and low or no cost money orders/cashier's checks
  - More than one or one set of NSF/ODs waived
- Acceptance of alternative identification information (such as Mexican consular ID)
- Acceptance of ITINs in lieu of SS #s (not as ID)
- Pathways for customers with Chex System 'activity' that is more than six months old (Restitution and fraud policies of individual institutions still apply).
- Clear disclosure of fees, rates, and procedures (in addition to all of the notifications that institutions are required to provide)
- Savings account option

---

meet the needs of all unbanked people, and that a diversity of institutions offering different products and services would be more conducive to meeting these needs on an individual basis.

One method of achieving this was to set forth the preferred criteria, such as a minimum opening deposit of $50 or less, and then allow for "exceptions" that would be transparent to preserve alternatives for the customer. This path was also used to determine that some institutions could charge a small (originally up to $6 per month) monthly maintenance fee. In 2011, the maximum allowable fee was increased to $10 per month, as larger institutions began charging more substantial monthly fees even for these Bank On accounts, arguing that changing regulations had required them to increase their fees. As mainstay partners in the initiative, this change was made to accommodate them.

Bank on S-KC also developed a set of criteria that financial institutions were strongly encouraged, but not required to offer:

Bank on S-KC was designed to be sustainable for financial institutions, not just as charity or simply an avenue to Community Reinvestment Act (CRA) credit, but as a legitimate business segment that financial institutions would

Box 3

> ### Characteristics of a Bank on S-KC Account
>
> - Financial incentives for at least some who open accounts at their institutions through Bank on Seattle – King County who also complete high-quality financial education
> - Programs that encourage savings (such as automatic savings programs)
> - Foreign remittances (at low or no cost)
> - Free online banking
> - Actively encourage and promote direct deposit
> - Accounts for those who have been on ChexSystems for less than six months on a case-by-case basis
> - Referrals to other participating institutions for Bank on Seattle–King County customers unable to open an account

want to compete for. Thus, Bank on S-KC chose not to develop one Bank on S-KC account that all participating banks and credit unions would have to offer. Instead, the product criteria represented a minimum acceptable standard with room for additional, attractive features. This approach subsequently led Bank on S-KC to emphasize transparency and outreach and communication, letting the public and Bank on S-KC's community partners know about the features and specific products offered by Bank on S-KC's financial institutions.

*Marketing and Outreach*
Getting the word out to the community about the program is a challenge many Bank On programs face. Trusted community partners are the backbone of the Bank on S-KC effort, providing credibility to the financial institutions and the program itself. To address this challenge, the Marketing and Outreach workgroup, led by a local community organization representative, used county demographics to target different localities, languages, and ethnic groups. A plan was developed to distribute outreach brochures through dozens of SKC ABC partners. Based on demographic research, the group was determined to translate and disseminate the outreach materials in 12 languages, in addition to English:

Banking on Opportunity
A Scan of the Evolving Field of Bank On Initiatives    US DEPARTMENT OF THE TREASURY    69
Office of Financial Education and Financial Access

- Amharic
- Cambodian
- Chinese
- Korean
- Laotian
- Russian
- Somali
- Spanish
- Tagalog
- Tigrinya
- Ukrainian
- Vietnamese

Bank on S-KC sought the services of a pro bono marketing firm to design the materials, including an outreach brochure, a poster, "buck slips" (for mailing inserts and other documents), and bus ads. The Seattle branch of the firm used by San Francisco, MRM Worldwide, was chosen because of their familiarity with the program, and the options they proposed for planning an advertising campaign. Bank on S-KC decided against a hard-hitting, anti-payday lender campaign used by some other cities – partly because of the lack of political will in taking on payday lenders locally—in favor of ads that promoted the benefits of opening an account. The firm eventually produced three separate bus ads that ran for four month intervals over a year.

An outreach brochure (Appendix 12) was created as a tool for both financial institutions and community groups to familiarize clients and customers with the program, explain why and how to open an account, and let people know which institutions were participating.

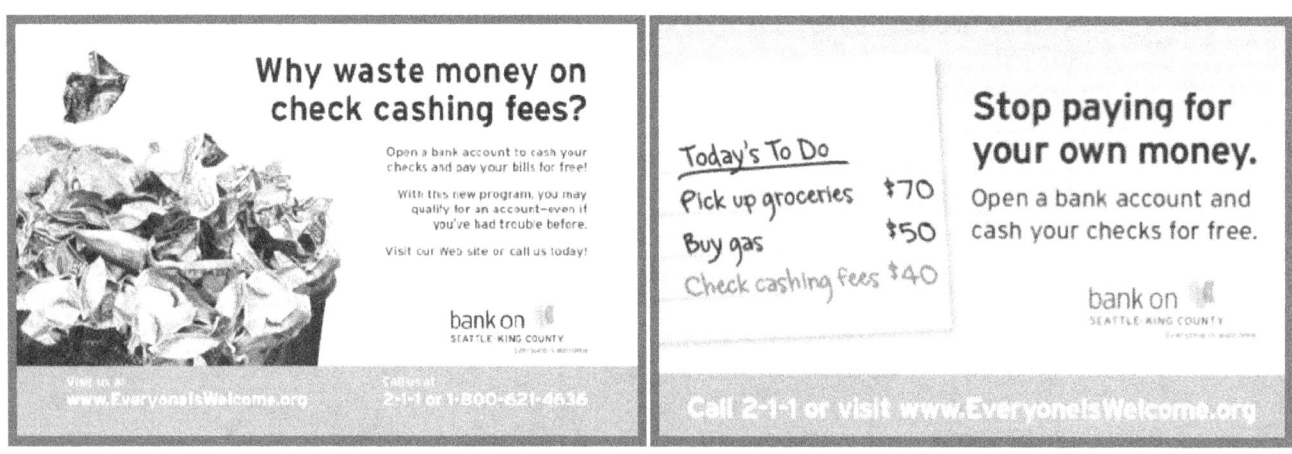

One of the primary challenges currently facing Bank on S-KC is maintaining the excitement and momentum of the campaign. For the first 18 months of the program, there were no staff dedicated solely to outreach. Once funds were available for an outreach position, Bank on S-KC was able to ramp up efforts by participating in community events, offering trainings and presentations to staff and clients of social service agencies, and contacting new community partners to spread the word. The Outreach Coordinator is alert to opportunities that foster direct relationships between financial partners and community groups and can help adapt to changing demographics and needs within the unbanked community, such as the need for translation into new languages.

*Budget and Resources*
In order to help pay for extensive outreach and marketing efforts, the financial institutions used a complex formula to determine contributions that balance the needs and requirements of both large and small institutions (See Appendix 13). The contribution plan was not overly burdensome to large institutions with dozens of branches within the County, nor was it prohibitively expensive for the smaller participating institutions with just a few branches. The formula required each institution to contribute an initial amount for participation, in addition to a set amount per branch, which decreased as the number of branches increased. Both large and small institutions viewed certain aspects of the plan as unfair, but for the initial phase of 2008-2010, all 22 participating institutions paid their share.[78]

These contributions totaled $185,000. The revenues paid for the printing of outreach materials, financial education brochures, and other promotional materials such as three different bus ads that ran for four months each, and some additional marketing, including Val-Pak coupons and advertising in a Spanish language newspaper.

The largest expenses of the program—leadership, coordination, and staffing—were donated by SKC ABC and the City. While the City continues to lead the initiative and set the agenda, a donated staff person from the SKC ABC provides ongoing coordination of meetings, acts as a liaison to financial institution representatives, responds to customer complaints, leads data collection and analysis, writes applications for funding, oversees marketing and media efforts, and supervises the work of the Outreach Coordinator and Financial Education Project Manager. SKC ABC staff also provides the leadership and staffing of the Financial Education Providers Network. It is only during the 2011-2012 phase that revenues raised from the financial institutions are being used to supplement staffing costs of SKC ABC.

Another substantial program cost is the King County 2-1-1 Community Information Line, which costs Bank on S-KC $10,000 for a two year period. King County 2-1-1 includes Bank on S-KC in its resource and referral service, and includes a message on its hold line offering assistance in finding an appropriate bank or credit union for callers. The Seattle Foundation, a local community foundation, provided the funds to secure 2-1-1 as the portal for Bank on S-KC. The Seattle Foundation also became a sponsor of the initiative, agreeing to serve as the fiscal sponsor to which financial institutions make their contributions. The fiscal sponsorship allows the program to raise funds as a non-profit organization.

Finally, the City of Seattle pays $99 per year for the Bank On program website, www.everyoneiswelcome.org, which is updated and maintained by staff from the SKC ABC. Bank on S-KC saves thousands of dollars in information technology costs by relying on an SKC ABC volunteer to develop, customize, monitor, and improve the software, and update databases when necessary. The volunteer initially spent a large amount of time in developing the website, but only needs to spend a few hours per week to maintain it.

*Data Tracking and Evaluation*
Since the program's launch, data tracking and evaluation have presented themselves as significant challenges. The data tracking work group was led by a representative from one of the largest financial institution partners, U.S. Bank. The large banks maintained that they would be unable to alter any of their account-tracking processes to accommodate Bank on S-KC reporting. The banks that were also participating in Bank on San Francisco stated that they would only be able to report the same set of data. Bank of America was not even able to report what it had in the San Francisco initiative due to a different technology platform. Many institutions, including the largest participating credit union, stated they were unable to "flag" the accounts, which would have allowed them to pull information about the requested fields.

---

78   The economic climate for financial institutions in mid-2007 was different than it is at present. Bank On S-KC launched at a time when financial institution support may have been easier to acquire but three years later, the Bank on S-KC is experiencing a greater challenge to garner the same financial resources that supported the initial effort.

Banking on Opportunity
A Scan of the Evolving Field of Bank On Initiatives     **US DEPARTMENT OF THE TREASURY**     71
Office of Financial Education and Financial Access

For the initial phase, the data committee established two underlying tracking agreements: only aggregate data would be reported publicly (no singling out of individual institutions), and each financial institution's data would be reported to the DFI. All institutions were asked to report on "previously unbanked" customers, which included anyone who did not have a checking or savings account at the time of opening the new account. This definition permitted customers to be included even if they did not ask specifically for "Bank on Seattle-King County," in part because many partners were using other names for their basic accounts.

The work group met with Matt Fellowes and then with Pew Charitable Trusts, who advocated for ambitious tracking and reporting in order to evaluate the impact and effectiveness of Bank on initiatives. Ultimately the work group recommended that financial institutions report extensive data, with the following caveat: "Participating financial institutions are expected to make a good faith effort to provide all of the recommended data elements in the recommended data set, although an institution's inability to do so will be considered and may not preclude participation in the initiative." The work group and key Bank on SKC leaders knew that it would be necessary to continue working after the launch with financial institutions on their tracking and reporting.

Finally, Bank on S-KC developed a list of data that would allow for an incisive analysis of performance. Measures included:

- Number of checking accounts opened during the quarter for previously unbanked customers
- Number of newly banked customers during the quarter who were on ChexSystems at the time of opening the account
- Total number of previously unbanked checking accounts currently open (cumulative)
- Average balance during the quarter of all open checking accounts
- Number of accounts that used direct deposit during the quarter
- Number of accounts that had a non-sufficient funds (NSF) charge and/or an overdraft (OD) during the quarter
- Total number of NSF and/or OD occurrences during the quarter
- Number of accounts that had one or more ATM/debit transactions during the quarter
- Total number of ATM/debit transactions during the quarter
- Number of accounts that were active during the quarter (defined as at least three deposits, withdrawals, or other activity)
- Number of accounts that were closed during the quarter
- Total number of previously unbanked customers' checking accounts closed (cumulatively since the inception of the program)

Financial institutions were also asked to report on the number of accounts closed and the reasons behind it, such as inactivity, excessive NSF/OD, customer request, or upgrade to other accounts. The reporting form also tracked the number and average balance of savings accounts, and requested the number of customers accessing home equity lines of credit, CDs, using online banking, and other products and services.

*Financial Education*
Financial education has always been an integral component of Bank on S-KC. The financial education workgroup, initially chaired by a representative from Apprisen Financial Advocates, subsequently evolved into a robust and growing Financial Education Providers Network (FEPN). Bank on S-KC partners recognized that many newly banked customers need financial knowledge and skills to successfully utilize their checking and savings accounts. Otherwise, those accounts could lead customers into even worse financial circumstances, with the accretion of overdraft fees and other unexpected fees. Therefore, one of the major goals of Bank on S-KC was to provide accessible, high quality financial education. However, program planners felt that requiring financial education as a precondition for an account was counterproductive. The solution was to create a network of financial education providers who would align their work with the Bank on S-KC to offer classes and one-on-one counseling for Bank On customers.

FEPN provides free, high quality financial education, particularly to underserved communities throughout King County. It makes the delivery of financial education more accessible, efficient, and effective by sharing resources and information, establishing quality standards, avoiding duplication of efforts, and jointly promoting financial education training opportunities. Furthermore, because community organizations and financial institutions have confidence in the quality of the education provided, this allows them to make referrals or offer incentives for people interested in improving their financial acumen. Over 20 financial education providers, listed in the www.everyoneiswelcome.org website, agreed to the following participation requirements:

- Accept an agreed-upon set of standards defining the elements of high quality financial education;
- Perform a self-assessment based on the standards, in order to determine where and how improvements need to be made within the organization;
- Develop an organizational plan to improve the quality of education provided and/or increase in access to free financial education;
- Share information about financial education programs and services among those in the network;
- Agree to be listed on the Bank on Seattle-King County website as a source of free financial education; and
- Help develop a system of evaluating effectiveness of methods and programs of financial education.

These financial education providers offer free classes, workshops, or one-on-one counseling to the public. They list their offerings through a locator tool on the www.everyoneiswelcome.org website, as well as on a calendar uploaded to the DFI website.

In one of its first activities, FEPN developed and adopted standards for curriculum content, adapted from standards advanced by Express Credit Union (Appendix 14). FEPN members conducted a self-assessment of their financial education curriculum based on those standards to identify where they needed to add curriculum or train staff in order to improve their financial education classes and counseling. FEPN has met monthly for two and a half years, hosting substantive professional development opportunities to improve members' understanding and capability of financial topics, such as: credit reports; medical debt; financial empowerment for people with disabilities; basic investment strategies; accessing public benefits, and many others. FEPN meetings also provide opportunities for members to share experiences, resources, and best practices, as well as to collaborate on projects. Agencies seeking financial educators for their clients and classes can find partners at these meetings.

In addition, as part of its initial recommendations, the Bank on S-KC Financial Education work group created a Financial Education brochure (Appendix 15) intended to be distributed by banking partners to new customers when they opened their accounts, a time considered to be a "teachable moment". The Financial Education brochure, available on the website, was translated and printed in the same 12 languages as the Outreach brochure. Community partners also use these brochures as a basic financial education resource.

Although the financial institutions decided not to use their pooled contributions to Bank on S-KC as incentive money for all customers who completed a series of financial education classes, four partners[79] decided to offer financial incentives to their own Bank on S-KC customers. These partners met separately, with Bank on S-KC staff, to develop the criteria that would need to be met for a customer to qualify for the incentive. FEPN then certified which providers would be able to issue the certificates.[80] The financial institution partners required that a qualifying financial education class must include the following standards:

1. The following topics covered by the FEPN's Financial Education Standards:
   - Financial Goal Setting
   - Controlling Your Money
   - Checking Accounts
   - Savings
   - Credit and Credit History
   - Credit Cards
   - Consumer Rights
2. At least eight hours of class time
3. A minimum of two separate class periods (e.g., four hours each)
4. Take-home resources and/or homework between classes
5. Testing of financial education knowledge acquired through these classes

79  Currently, three partners are offering the incentive.
80  American Financial Solutions, Apprisen Financial Advocates, CARES of Washington, ClearPoint Credit Counseling Solutions, Consumer Education and Training Services (CENTS), El Centro de la Raza, HomeSight, Hopelink, International District Housing Alliance, Jennifer Beach Foundation, Lutheran Community Service, Multi-Service Center, Neighborhood House, Parkview Services, Port Jobs, Seattle Goodwill, United Indians of All Tribes Foundation, Urban League of Metropolitan Seattle, Washington C.A.S.H., Washington Working Families Prosperity Center, YMCA Young Adult Services, and YWCA—Economic Resilience Program.

Banking on Opportunity
A Scan of the Evolving Field of Bank On Initiatives    US DEPARTMENT OF THE TREASURY    73
Office of Financial Education and Financial Access

The incentives offered by the partners vary. Each customer who successfully completes the minimum education requirements and obtains a certificate from the Bank on S-KC is offered

- $100 from Banner Bank
- $100 from HomeStreet Bank if the customer maintains a checking for a minimum of three months with a positive balance
- a $50 matching deposit into a 6 month Savers Certificate from Verity Credit Union for each member who is in good standing with Verity at the certificate maturity date in order to withdraw the $50 matching deposit.[81]

*Training of Branch Personnel*

Since most of Bank on S-KC financial partners do not consider Seattle as a stand-alone market, it was important for the initiative to be countywide, especially since the target populations the program hoped to serve—immigrants, refugees and lower income residents— are concentrated in neighborhoods in south Seattle and south King County. For this countywide initiative, the 22 participating banks and credit unions represented more than 400 branches with thousands of personnel. Ensuring that all personnel) were knowledgeable about the campaign and enthusiastic about welcoming new banking customers on a continuing basis posed a significant challenge.

Under the leadership of a credit union partner's Training Manager, Bank on S-KC created a 1.5-hour presentation designed to familiarize branch managers with the purpose and requirements of the program, the standards of the accounts that could be offered, and the features of the accounts that each financial institution actually offers as part of Bank on S-KC. The training included a PowerPoint presentation and handouts that were designed to be used in the training of their own frontline branch personnel. Furthermore, under the guidance of another credit union partner's Manager of Public Relations, Bank on S-KC produced a video featuring Mayor Nickels and Councilmember Clark, that introduced and explained Bank on S-KC. This video was later posted on www.youtube.com.[82] In addition, former President Clinton taped a video in support of the program that was also used in training and outreach. Financial Institutions use these training materials to train their own staff. Therefore the frequency of trainings varies from institution to institution.

*The Bank on Seattle-King County Launch*

On September 22, 2008, Bank on S-KC was officially launched at a City Hall luncheon, sponsored by the Federal Reserve Bank and FDICand featuring then-Mayor Greg Nickels, Councilmember Sally Clark, Washington State Representative Eric Pettigrew, DFI Director Scott Jarvis, and Urban League's (one of SKC ABC's partners) Executive Direction James Kelly. Sixteen banks and six credit unions signed on as participating financial institutions for the initial two-year phase through the end of 2010.

Following the launch, a Coordinating Committee was formed to provide leadership and monitor fund expenditures. The Committee consists of representatives from large banks, community banks, credit unions, and community partners, as well as from all sponsoring agencies. In 2009, Bank on S-KC added two sponsors, FDIC and King County government, and their representatives also joined the Coordinating Committee. This Committee meets quarterly, or more often when necessary to make key program decisions.

Challenges Faced by Bank on Seattle-King County

*Diversity of Financial Institutions*

At the outset, there was some concern about how such a diverse group of financial institutions—large banks, small banks, and credit unions—could agree on universal parameters for a common program. However, ensuring involvement of representatives from all types of institutions in the development of the initiative helped ensure buy-in with the purpose, principles, and framework of the program. No one institution or product could meet the financial needs of all unbanked and underbanked people in Seattle and King County. By having a diversity of institutions and clarity on the products and services each offers, Bank on S-KC could match customers with the institution that could best meet their needs and preferences.

Moreover, Bank on S-KC embraced the notion of voluntary cooperation in order to accommodate these competing constituencies. There were no MOUs signed between the program and the financial institutions, but

81  It is too soon to have meaningful results from the incentive programs. While about 500 certificates were provided to community partners, data has not yet been collected on how many have been deposited into financial institutions.
82  The link to the video is the following: http://www.youtube.com/watch?v=77prYFuW8iQ.

74    **US DEPARTMENT OF THE TREASURY**
Office of Financial Education and Financial Access        Banking on Opportunity
A Scan of the Evolving Field of Bank On Initiatives

rather an understanding—cemented by a substantial financial contribution—that participants would abide by the rules of the program, to the best of their abilities.

For example, one requirement of the initiative was that each financial institution was required to offer a clear, written explanation of fees and rates to each newly banked customer. All institutions, of course, provided the required official notifications and disclosures, but Bank on S-KC also wanted an understandable and readable explanation to be given the newly banked customers. Bank on S-KC provided a template (Appendix 16) that could be customized for each participating institution. However, only six of the participating institutions actually created a document using the provided template to use with their customers. Other institutions had their own notices, which they believed complied with this Bank on S-KC requirement.

*Data Reporting and Tracking*

Similar to many other Bank On campaigns, one of the most significant ongoing challenges confronting Bank on S-KC is the inability or unwillingness of participating financial institutions – especially the large banks – to report all of the agreed-upon data. As outlined above, the Tracking and Evaluation Committee, based on the advice of the Pew Fellow, recommended collecting an ambitious array of data that would help evaluate and analyze the effectiveness of the program. However, because of the existing tracking systems, especially in larger institutions, some institutions were unable to "flag" follow Bank on S-KC accounts. Furthermore, because most of the institutions did not have a product named "Bank on Seattle-King County," it posed a challenge for them to identify all previously unbanked customers in their reporting. This was especially the case for the large banks, some of which could only report the number of new accounts; a few others could also report an average balance, but nothing else.

As a result, the collected data is not complete because many of the larger banks declined to include any information on numerous categories. Based on the initial agreement, Bank on S-KC may only report aggregate data, which makes the missing pieces even more problematic. In an effort to ameliorate the situation, upon the completion of the initial commitment through the end of 2010, Bank on S-KC has implemented a streamlined, online reporting system. This new quarterly reporting plan will request the following data on the accounts:

- Total number of checking and savings accounts opened quarterly, and cumulatively
- Average balances during the quarter
- Number of accounts with an NSF and/or OD during the quarter

Bank on S-KC anticipates improved compliance and will be able to compile the data more efficiently through the website database.

Despite the reporting limitations encountered during the initiative's first two years, Bank on S-KC has documented the opening of over 54,000 new accounts for previously unbanked customers. As of the 2011 first Quarter, checking accounts had an average balance of $652, and savings accounts had an average balance of $932.

*Funding Challenges*

Moving forward beyond the initial commitment period, Bank on S-KC faces challenges in raising funds for the ongoing operational support necessary to ensure a successful initiative. Funds are needed to update and reprint outreach and educational materials, to support staffing costs, and for marketing and outreach to maintain momentum. Although the original Financial Assessment was approved for the 2011-12 campaign, the partners also agreed that contributions were voluntary, and more limited monetary sums could be complemented with in-kind support. For example, one bank partner is re-designing outreach materials to supplement its financial contribution.

*Training and Awareness of Financial Institution Personnel*

For a large Bank on initiative, one of the major challenges is to ensure that all participating financial institution personnel know about the program and the specific products and features offered by their own institution that are aligned with Bank on. During the first two years of the initiative, 2-1-1 received about 50 calls from customers who were told by bank or credit union personnel that they had never heard of the program. However, so far in 2011, no complaints have yet been reported by 2-1-1. Bank on S-KC has trained trainers from all participating financial institutions and has offered to provide training directly to branch personnel, but most of the financial institutions prefer to do the training themselves. They acknowledge, however, that it is difficult to keep the program at the forefront, as their frontline staff have so many other products and programs that they need to know about.

### Change in Political Leadership

Bank on S-KC has successfully weathered the political challenge of a change in mayoral leadership. Along with Councilmember Clark, Former Mayor Nickels provided the high-level political leadership necessary to convene the financial institutions in the initial stages. However, steadfast support from the City Council and the City of Seattle Human Services Department allowed the program to transition smoothly to a new Mayor. Councilmember Clark notes that the challenge for the future will be to determine how to best sustain the program, and whether it would be preferable if City government had less of a direct leadership role, allowing Bank on S-KC to transition into becoming its own distinct non-profit entity. On the other hand, Human Services staff believes it may be difficult to sustain the initiative without the political leadership and convening role of the City.

## Innovative Strategies and Best Practices

### EveryoneIsWelcome website

Bank on S-KC adopted the Bank on San Francisco tagline "Everyone Is Welcome" as its website name (partly because "BankonSeattleKingCounty" was deemed too long), and initially used the San Francisco "look and feel" to build its own website. Over time, Bank on S-KC substantially adapted the site in order to meet the needs of its partners and customers. A pro bono technical expert developed and customized a locator tool and map, simplified the language and look of the website, and added numerous enhancements and resources. Most importantly, the following added tools increased the utility of the site and transparency of the products for customers.

- Bank and Credit Union Profiles

    Each financial partner completed a template delineating the contours of the products and features of their "Bank on S-KC" account and other information relevant to customers. This "Profile" can be accessed from the website's home page, allowing customers to view the fees charged on the accounts and any additional features they might need, such as the availability and cost of foreign wire transfers; the cost of money orders and cashier's checks; and opportunities for incentive and savings programs.

- Comparison Chart

    Transparency is a fundamental tenet to providing trustworthy access to affordable financial products. In an effort to streamline a customer's efforts to find the best alternatives for his or her needs, Bank on S-KC created a Comparison Chart (available a click away from the home page) that lists the costs and products offered by each financial partner. This Comparison Chart was designed—at the request of community partners—to be downloadable for easy reference for case managers working with clients to find the most appropriate bank or credit union.

- Financial Education Providers

    The website is designed to be a destination for people seeking financial education resources, which is a crucial component of the initiative. Contact information for the agencies in the Financial Education Providers Network is listed, as well as a link to the DFI's Financial Education calendar, which provides the dates and times of free classes offered. Most importantly, the site includes a customized locator tool that allows customers to choose topics, location, language, audience, and type of setting (workshop, one-on-one, or classroom) for the financial education and counseling that they seek.

- Additional Links

    The site provides additional useful information, including sections on "How to Avoid Overdraft Fees," "Affordable Alternatives to Payday Loans," and "Helpful Links and Resources." The outreach and education materials have been translated into 13 languages, and allare available for download from the website. The websites of the community partners can also be accessed through the links on the homepage.

The website is used as the primary tool for 2-1-1 and other case managers to help them recommend appropriate financial institutions for customers. It is also directly accessible to the public, and receives approximately 1,500 visitors each month.

*Financial Education Providers Network*

As mentioned earlier, the Financial Education Providers Network (FEPN), led by the SKC ABC, represents a best practice of Bank on S-KC, providing a key systems change in King County. This network provides significant incentives to community groups to stay involved with the campaign and promote financial access and education to their constituencies on a professional manner. The high quality monthly training workshops and opportunities for networking is beneficial for case managers and financial educators who work directly with clients. FEPN serves as a vehicle to break down the silos of agencies and lets them establish collaborative relationships to increase the financial capability of their clients. FEPN has evolved from a loose collection of financial education providers to a more structured entity, providing guidance on financial coaching and education for a wide range of community partners. The network provides ongoing opportunities for professional development and sharing of promising practices. Some of the most active members of the network include Hopelink, Urban League, YWCA, and three non-profit credit counseling agencies.

*Small Dollar Loans*

A major goal of Bank on S-KC is to provide affordable credit opportunities to unbanked and underbanked customers, and help them avoid high rates charged by payday lenders. Consequently, Bank on S-KC formed a working group on Credit Alternatives soon after launching. This group met throughout 2009 with numerous bank and credit union partners and community organization representatives to establish the basic criteria for "small dollar loans" within Bank on S-KC. The objective was to increase access to fair, responsible loans that were sustainable for lenders. While open to loans that would charge up to 36 percent APR, as the discussions continued, it became clear that institutions that planned to offer a loan would not charge more than 18 percent APR, so that became the standard. After extensive negotiations among interested parties, the following criteria were established:

Product Requirements:
- Loan minimum of $500 or less (No maximum limit required)
- APR not to exceed 18%
- Payment terms beyond one paycheck cycle for closed-end loans (such as, 90 days, or one month for every $100 borrowed)
- No prepayment penalties
- Closed-end loans should be paid in full before another advance
- Streamlined underwriting (determined by each institution, but lenders are encouraged not to use an arbitrary FICO score cut-off, and to approve loans within 24 hours)

Recommended, but non-required features are:
- Participation in financial education
- Automatic savings component (whereby a portion of each loan repayment goes into a savings account)
- Direct deposit
- Payment terms beyond one paycheck cycle for open-ended loans

Three financial partners—a major bank and two credit unions--committed to offering this loan (although one has since dropped out of Bank on S-KC after being absorbed by another credit union). Several others have expressed interest in developing a loan product aligned with Bank on S-KC criteria. These loans are described and promoted through the website and community outreach.[83]

Program Impact and Systems Change

*Impact from Strong Relationships*

One of the most important positive impacts is the improved, strong relationships among financial institutions, the City, and community partners that were fostered by Bank on S-KC. Financial institutions have become integral partners in the work of the SKC ABC and its efforts to increase access to high-quality, financial education and financial empowerment services. Some financial institutions have participated in workshops for the Financial

---

83  The small dollar loan product is relatively new at the time of writing this report and there have been no data yet reported from the banks on the success of these loans.

Education Providers Network, and several have partnered with community groups to present financial education workshops or to open accounts for clients in classes or at events. Some of the institutions that offer financial incentives form partnerships with community organizations that award certificates to their clients after completion of the prescribed financial education classes.

Many partners—such as community organizations and financial institutions—have sponsored or participated in community-based events designed to reach out to and provide residents with a wide variety of financial empowerment services and connect them to providers. These events have included a Your Money Helpline phone-a-thon, Financial Planning Day, and Financial Fitness Day, which took place during Financial Literacy Month. Connections between financial institutions and SKC ABC have also facilitated work on foreclosure prevention, such as promoting partners who offer mortgages to participate in community events geared towards connecting homeowners with their lenders, housing counselors, and pro bono attorneys.

In addition, the City of Seattle has benefitted from a closer relationship with financial partners. For example, when the City recently wanted more housing for victims of domestic violence, they were able to use their strong relationships with financial institution partners to broker conversations about possible funding assistance. Moreover, the City has incorporated Bank on S-KC into its one-stop public benefits initiative, PeoplePoint, and now screens residents seeking State- or City-administered benefits on whether they use check cashers and if they have a bank account.

*Systems Change*

A significant system change that Bank on S-KC created is a pathway for people with troubled banking histories to join the financial mainstream. In the past, people who were placed on ChexSystems would have been denied the opportunity to open a bank account for five years. Under the protocol established by Bank on S-KC, banks and credit unions agreed to open accounts for people who were placed on the system over six months ago and if they met the institution's fraud and restitution policies.

Significantly, some institutions agreed to go beyond Bank on S-KC's minimum criteria and consider opening accounts even when customers had not made restitution or had been placed on ChexSystems for an incident that occurred less than six months previously. In fact, the loosening of the standards for opening Bank on accounts is one of the major changes noted by financial institution representatives (see below). For those financial institutions that reported on this indicator, 40 percent of their newly banked customers through Bank on S-KC were on ChexSystems at the time of opening their accounts. Bank on S-KC takes pride in living up to its tagline, Everyone Is Welcome. Most of the difficult-to-bank cases are referred to SKC ABC, which has been able to connect virtually everyone with a financial institution that provides an appropriate financial product, even if the customer does not meet Bank on S-KC criteria. Only customers who are listed in ChexSystems for fraudulent activities are turned away.

Another important systems change is that the Bank on S-KC spawned the widely regarded FEPN (described above), which grew out of the initiative's emphasis on financial education. FEPN has promoted the development of financial coaching and provides opportunities for community partners to share effective practices. As a result of Bank on S-KC, King County now has a cohesive system of financial education providers with opportunities for cross-collaboration and skills enhancement, offering people access to high-quality education opportunities. In part because of FEPN, SKC ABC has been able to develop a Financial Empowerment workshop series designed for agencies interested in embedding financial education and financial empowerment services into their service delivery. The workshops, and follow up technical assistance, raise awareness about the importance of mainstream banking and the Bank on S-KC initiative, and provide resources and tools that agencies can use when working with their clients. Bank on S-KC, FEPN, and SKC ABC are systematically increasing knowledge about the capacity to provide financial empowerment.

Financial Institution Perspectives

*Why participate?*

From the perspective of financial institutions, what makes Bank on S-KC successful is the community involvement. This initiative provided an unprecedented opportunity for financial institutions to collaborate with a large network of community groups serving a traditionally hard to reach population. As Todd Pietzsch of BECU explains, "This program reaches the unbanked in ways we couldn't by leveraging the trust and credibility of non-profits." For credit unions and small community banks, their missions aligned perfectly and Bank on S-KC provided an effective way to reach out to ease the burdens of struggling community members. They were "appalled" to learn how much payday lenders and check cashers charged. For larger institutions, the regulatory imperative of community reinvestment and civic responsibility is paramount. One major national bank partner, Courtney Jinjika of KeyBank, commented that Bank on S-KC provided the opportunity for the bank to learn why people were unbanked and opened an avenue to attract that population to their appropriate products. Thus, both the desire to serve the community, as well as the opportunity to increase their business through new consumer accounts, drives their enthusiasm to participate. As Mr. Pietzsch elaborated, "If you are doing this right, these are people who will eventually need a car, a new home, and you will have a relationship with them."

All of the financial institutions agreed that the greatest benefit to them and the most effective way for institutions to get the most out of the program is to take advantage of the partnerships offered by community organizations. Bank on S-KC's Outreach Coordinator introduces financial institution branch managers to nearby community partners to facilitate direct relationships. Many of the financial institutions are eager to go onsite to the community groups to educate clients about banking and opening accounts. Financial partners have been able to take advantage of the financial empowerment community events sponsored by SKC ABC, and in one case, a partner was thrilled to open ten accounts in one day for previously unbanked customers. Some of the financial institutions have strategically utilized Bank on S-KC in their work with businesses. Kathy Williams of HomeStreet points out that when their business development account representatives talk to small businesses (for example, restaurateurs), they now have a vehicle to offer accounts to all of the business's employees, allowing them to implement company-wide direct deposit.

*Products and Services*

One of the most significant impacts that Bank on S-KC had on the banking community was insisting that the Mexican Matricula card be used as an acceptable form of identification. In addition, many institutions loosened their standards on approving accounts for people on ChexSystems, as well as agreeing to waive one set of overdraft fees. Some financial institutions were also motivated to lower their minimum opening deposit requirement, realizing that an initial commitment should be small until the customer grew to trust and use the new account. A few began offering incentives for customers to complete a prescribed course of financial education.

Since the financial institutions developed the minimum criteria for participation themselves, there was a largely enthusiastic buy-in with the final recommendations. Most agree that having some flexibility within the criteria (e.g., range of opening deposit; level of monthly fee) is positive, allowing for a diversity of institutions to join the initiative, especially larger institutions that have less flexibility in accommodating local initiatives. However, some of the community banks and credit unions would have preferred to require institutions to offer an account with no monthly maintenance fees at all.

*Challenges*

Financial institutions point to data tracking and reporting as their biggest challenge. Many of the larger institutions had difficulty in flagging accounts for previously unbanked customers and needed to report numbers based on only a particular type of account opened in low-income neighborhoods (acknowledging that their reporting was thus not entirely accurate for Bank on S-KC accounts). Furthermore, many could only report basic information about the accounts rather than all of the data that had initially been agreed upon. Smaller institutions also had to make adjustments that were difficult, and some did not have the technological infrastructure capable of reporting all of the data elements. The institutions are hopeful that the new, streamlined online reporting will make the process easier.

Even among institutions that have been closely tracking their data, some have not analyzed the data to determine if the Bank on S-KC accounts are profitable or breaking even. From the reported data, the accounts appear to have a higher rate of overdrafts. However, since only a few of the financial institutions report overdraft information, it is difficult to determine the validity of this observation. Financial institutions acknowledge that they earn money with the customer's use of debit cards, but some are focused on providing these accounts as a service to the community, without specifically looking at the bottom line.

One partner pointed to the importance of obtaining "buy-in" from the highest levels of the financial institution. When serving the unbanked population is not established as part of the bank culture by those in leadership positions, frontline staff often lack the will and ability to market the program. It can be difficult to convince someone to become banked just because "it is the right thing to do." Bank executives must know how the program works, what their obligations are, and who will be managing it in order to ensure for successful implementation. Transparency in the initiative was helpful to bring them on board.

Many of the partners anticipate that federal regulatory changes may limit the ability of some institutions to continue offering free checking accounts. Although these changes may primarily affect larger banks, they could test the limits of what is acceptable as an "affordable" mainstream account.

## Community Partner Perspectives

More than 100 community agencies have worked with Bank on S-KC in some fashion to disseminate program details and materials to their constituencies. Some of these groups have handed out materials, while others have worked closely with the Financial Education Providers Network and SKC ABC to integrate financial education and counseling into their one-on-one case management systems.

Community partners have been integral to the success of the Bank on S-KC initiative by increasing public awareness of the opportunities, reaching specific population groups – such as immigrants and refugees– that otherwise would be very difficult to reach, and lending credibility to financial institutions that their clients might not otherwise trust. Similarly, the outreach for the program has increased the visibility and credibility of some of the community partners. In general, community groups are thrilled to have an option for their clients that allow them access into the financial mainstream and give them an opportunity to save money. As Audi Ritz of American Financial Solutions states, Bank on S-KC is "another tool in the toolbox to help people reach their financial goals." Tracy Greene of Hopelink has used the financial incentive as part of her financial education curriculum, encouraging students to use their incentives to open savings accounts. Staff from King County 2-1-1 saw many of their callers having financial problems as a result of involvement with payday lenders, allowing for a "natural partnership" with Bank on S-KC to form.

The community partners themselves have benefitted from being able to pool resources, expand their networks, and share best practices, including financial education curriculum, around financial empowerment issues. They are grateful to have a network of high quality service providers they can trust in referring their clients to. They also point to how Bank on S-KC worked with agencies with diverse viewpoints to bring a variety of social and cultural issues to the table, including addressing the needs of immigrants, refugees, and people with a variety of disabilities.

Some of the improvements they would like to see include:

- Explicit, transparent options explained (e.g., what advantage does an account with a monthly fee have over the free ones?);
- More flexibility for people who are on ChexSystems and cannot pay back the fees they owe; and
- More short-term, low interest, small dollar loans (including employers using payroll deductions for credit-building loans).

One of the primary challenges for community partners is to keep the initiative front-and-center and maintain the momentum of the campaign. After the initial excitement and before Bank on S-KC hired an Outreach Coordinator, it was more difficult to maintain partner engagement in the ongoing discussions of the implementation. The Outreach Coordinator is working with the partners to build meaningful relationships that reinforce the value of the initiative.

Next Steps for Bank on Seattle-King County

*Making Connections*

Bank on S-KC has been a catalyst to integrating financial empowerment initiatives into the poverty reduction strategies of the City of Seattle, adding a significant component to the work of HSD. Bank on S-KC collaborates with the City's PeoplePoint initiative, which offers a one-stop access to public benefits. The collaboration allows for the Bank On initiative to be incorporated into the PeoplePoint electronic benefits screening tool. In addition, Bank On is an essential feature of the SKC ABC's financial empowerment workshop series offered to social service case managers throughout the county, and used to raise awareness and understanding of financial issues. These workshops have helped connect these disparate networks and systems and have begun the process of embedding financial empowerment throughout the local social services system. Bank on S-KC is prominently featured in the series and provides some of the tools and resources the case managers need to help clients improve their financial situations.

*Bank on Washington*

As the first and largest "Bank On" campaign in the state of Washington, Bank on S-KC has been a leader and moving force in the effort to create a Bank on Washington initiative, with Diana Stone, Director of SKC ABC, serving as Co-Chair of the statewide effort. As local campaigns have begun to sprout across Washington, many statewide and national financial institutions have been clamoring for a coordinated campaign to standardize criteria and avoid duplication of efforts. Under the auspices of the statewide Washington Asset Building Coalition, a Bank on Washington Initiative Manager has been hired to plan this statewide coordination effort. Since many of the local campaigns are already using Bank on S-KC's model, many of the major aspects of Bank on S-KC will probably be replicated for Bank on Washington. For example, it is likely the minimum criteria will follow closely to those already established by Bank on S-KC, and that the marketing materials to bedeveloped will utilize much of the same content and general designs as the Bank on S-KC brochures. In addition, Bank on S-KC has made its website software, including the two locator tools, free and available nationally, and anticipates they will be used statewide. Finally, the online reporting form developed will also likely be the basis for the reporting required under Bank on Washington.

## Appendix 8: Success!  Newly Banked Customers Tell Their Stories

Major Bank Customer Carmen

A $500 minimum balance may not seem unreasonable to many affluent customers, but it's a daunting monthly sum to maintain for a hard-working house cleaner. When Carmen's hours were reduced, she could no longer afford minimal fees on her bank account and cancelled it. For more than a year, she struggled without a checking account, asking employers to pay in cash. When she started a job that paid her with checks, she asked her boyfriend to cash them whenever he could. She had no opportunities to save her money in a secure place, and saw no other options. Sitting on the bus on the way to work in the summer of 2010, Carmen saw an ad declaring, "Banking for Everyone: Open a bank account today!"  It promised "no minimum balance."  Most significantly, when she went to the website, she learned that the bank would accept an ITIN, instead of a social security number, which allowed her to open an account legally, without any fear.

Carmen reports that she has found a very welcoming branch of a major national bank that has provided her with a debit card and a free account that encourages her to start saving.  She is trying to save 10% of each check, even if it's just $10, to begin saving for emergencies.  She has already saved $200 in her second account, and she declares, "It's wonderful to have the freedom to be independent with my own account."

Community Bank Customer Michael

"Sometimes people just need a second chance to do the right thing," says Michael in explaining how Bank on Seattle-King County offered him a lifeline when he most needed it.  Michael faced a series of catastrophic events that snowballed to cause a perfect storm of financial instability.  In 2005, Michael, a college-educated corporate employee working in the account and finance sector, was still married and had good credit that allowed him to purchase a condo in downtown Seattle. After completing a degree in multi-media web design, Michael sought to switch careers but was unable to find another job in his new field. When he and his wife divorced shortly afterwards, he lost the condo and began bouncing between apartments, borrowing money from relatives and couch-surfing with friends. Eventually, he had nowhere else to go and ended up living at homeless shelters.

Not surprisingly, as Michael tried to make ends meet, he began taking out payday loans.  Unfortunately, his efforts to pay them off and break what he calls a "disastrous cycle" took a ruinous turn.  Unbeknownst to him, the payday lenders were demanding payment automatically at his bank, even when he did not have the funds to cover the withdrawals. Thus, each loan created a cascade of bank fees--which he didn't have money to repay—causing the bank to close his account. With this history of unpaid fees, Michael was unable to open a new checking account, even when he returned to work and attempted to rebuild his economic security.

Michael spent the next several years paying check cashers hundreds of dollars to cash his pay checks and pay his bills.  In late 2009, sitting on a bus, he noticed the ads for Bank on Seattle-King County and reached out for help. One of the community bank partners offered him that second chance, opening a checking account that prevented unintentional overdrafts, but provided him with a debit card. He sees the debit card as the most valuable part of having an account, as he needs it to register for classes he is taking and to purchase materials for the classes online. Although he is still working on digging himself out of debt, he gratefully acknowledges that "having a relationship with a bank is the first step in getting back on my feet." His community bank has been very welcoming, and despite the inconvenience of very few branches, he intends to stick with them, as he regains his financial legs with his new job.

## Appendix 9: Seattle-King County Case Study Sources

Bank on Seattle-King County, www.everyoneiswelcome.org
www.JoinBankOn.org

### Interviews

*Customers:*
KeyBank Customer Carmen, April 25, 2011
HomeStreet Bank Customer Michael, April 25, 2011

*Bank on Seattle-King County staff:*
Alice Coday, April 27, 2011
Jerry DeGrieck, April 25, 2011
Jennifer McAdam, April 27, 2011

*Political Leadership:*
Sally Clark, April 29, 2011

*Financial Institution Partners:*
Michael Dotson, Bank of America, April 29, 2011
Courtney Jinjika, KeyBank, April 27, 2011
Todd Pietzsch, BECU, April 26, 2011
Bev Roach, Union Bank (formerly Frontier Bank), April 26, 2011
Kathy Williams, HomeStreet Bank, April 27, 2011

*Community Partners:*
Jane Bloom, Parkview Services, April 27, 2011
Dana Easterling, May 4, 2011
Audi Ritz, American Financial Solutions, April 25, 2011
Tracy Greene, Hopelink, April 28, 2011

Contacts

Diana Stone
Director of Initiatives, Seattle-King County Asset-Building Collaborative
dstone@skcabc.org
206-275-1811

Jerry DeGrieck
Public Health and Policy Advisor
City of Seattle, Human Services Department
Jerry.degrieck@seattle.gov
206-684-0684

Alice Coday
Project Manager, Seattle-King County Asset Building Collaborative
acoday@skcabc.org
206-973-7474

Jennifer McAdam
Bank on Seattle-King County Outreach Coordinator
jmcadam@skcabc.org
253-297-0482

## Appendix 10: Initial Invitation to Banks

City of Seattle

Dear Bank Representative,                                    January 11, 2008

We are pleased to invite you to join the City of Seattle, the Federal Reserve Bank of San Francisco and the Washington State Department of Financial Institutions to develop and implement an initiative to provide affordable financial services to low-income residents of Seattle and King County.

The Brookings Institution estimates that there are approximately 52,000 households in Seattle and King County without checking accounts. These households pay up to $800 in unnecessary fees for cashing checks each year. We want to help you reach this untapped market and help "unbanked" residents of Seattle and King County keep more of what they earn and start on a pathway to improved financial success.

Several banks, credit unions and the Seattle – King County Asset Building Collaborative are already working with us on this effort. We are now urging all banks and credit unions in Seattle and King County who are interested in meeting the financial needs of low-income and working people to join us as we move forward.

If you would like to participate in this important effort, or if you have any questions, please contact any of the staff listed on the attached information.

To learn more about our efforts, you are also welcome to join a special one-day work session on Thursday, January 31, 2008. Thanks to the generosity of the William J. Clinton Foundation, several representatives from the Bank on San Francisco initiative, including San Francisco City Treasurer José Cisneros, will be in Seattle to share what they have learned helping more than 11,000 low-income San Francisco residents access mainstream financial services. Registration information is included on the attachment.

We look forward to working with you.

Sincerely,

Greg Nickels
Mayor of Seattle

Scott Jarvis
Director of the Washington State
Dept. of Financial Institutions

Sally Clark
Seattle City Councilmember

Mark A. Gould
Senior Vice President and
Seattle Branch Manager
Federal Reserve Bank of San Francisco

## Appendix 11: Initial Invitation to Credit Unions

City of Seattle

WASHINGTON STATE
DEPARTMENT OF
FINANCIAL
INSTITUTIONS

Dear Credit Union Representative,                                        January 11, 2008

We are pleased to invite you to join the City of Seattle, the Federal Reserve Bank of San Francisco and the Washington State Department of Financial Institutions to develop and implement an initiative to provide affordable financial services to low-income residents of Seattle and King County.

The Brookings Institution estimates that there are approximately 52,000 households in Seattle and King County without checking accounts. These households pay up to $800 in unnecessary fees for cashing checks each year. We want to help you reach this untapped market and help "unbanked" residents of Seattle and King County keep more of what they earn and start on a pathway to improved financial success.

Several banks, credit unions and the Seattle – King County Asset Building Collaborative are already working with us on this effort. We are now urging all banks and credit unions in Seattle and King County who are interested in meeting the financial needs of low-income and working people to join us as we move forward.

If you would like to participate in this important effort, or if you have any questions, please contact any of the staff listed on the attached information.

To learn more about our efforts, you are also welcome to join a special one-day work session on Thursday, January 31, 2008. Thanks to the generosity of the William J. Clinton Foundation, several representatives from the Bank on San Francisco initiative, including San Francisco City Treasurer José Cisneros, will be in Seattle to share what they have learned helping more than 11,000 low-income San Francisco residents access mainstream financial services. Registration information is included on the attachment.

We look forward to working with you.

Sincerely,

Greg Nickels
Mayor of Seattle

Scott Jarvis
Director of the Washington State
Dept. of Financial Institutions

Sally Clark
Seattle City Councilmember

Mark A. Gould
Senior Vice President and
Seattle Branch Manager
Federal Reserve Bank of San Francisco

## Appendix 12: Outreach Brochure

Bank on Seattle-King County is working with area banks and credit unions to help you open an account and keep more of your money.

- Using check cashers or buying money orders?
  Open an account today. Cash your checks and pay your bills for free.

- Don't have a lot of money?
  Depending on the bank or credit union you go to, you may need as little as $5 to open an account. Most will open an account for $50 or less, although a few may require up to $100 to open an account.

- How much will an account cost?
  Most participating banks and credit unions offer checking accounts with no monthly fees. A few charge a low monthly fee.

- Need to spend all of your money?
  You don't have to keep a minimum amount of money in your account each month to keep it open.

- Troubled banking history?
  If you've had a bank account closed or you've bounced checks more than six months ago, you may still be eligible for an account.

> For more information about Bank on Seattle-King County, visit www.EveryoneIsWelcome.org or call 2-1-1 or 1-800-621-4636.

Open a free or low-cost checking account and a savings account at any of these Bank on Seattle-King County participating financial institutions:

Bank of America
Banner Bank
BECU
Cathay Bank
Chase
City Bank
Columbia Bank
Express Credit Union
Frontier Bank
HomeStreet Bank
KeyBank
Pacific International Bank
Plaza Bank
Seattle Metropolitan Credit Union
Seattle Bank
United Commercial Bank
U.S. Bank
Verity Credit Union
Viking Bank
Watermark Credit Union
Wells Fargo Bank
Woodstone Credit Union

**bank on**
SEATTLE-KING COUNTY
Everyone is welcome

## CASH YOUR CHECKS FOR FREE
Now everyone can open a checking account.

For more information about Bank on Seattle-King County, visit www.EveryoneIsWelcome.org or call 2-1-1.

### What is Bank on Seattle-King County?

Bank on Seattle-King County is an initiative to help anyone without a bank account find affordable financial services. Bank on Seattle-King County is sponsored by the City of Seattle, FDIC, the Federal Reserve Bank of San Francisco, King County, The Seattle Foundation, the Seattle-King County Asset Building Collaborative, and the Washington State Department of Financial Institutions.

> For more information about Bank on Seattle-King County, visit www.EveryoneIsWelcome.org or call 2-1-1 or 1-800-621-4636. On our website, to help you figure out which bank or credit union will best meet your needs, click on "Find a Bank or Credit Union" under "How Do I Open an Account."

**bank on**
SEATTLE-KING COUNTY
Everyone is welcome

### How to open your own account:

- Find a participating bank or credit union near you.
  Check the list of financial institutions in this brochure or online at www.EveryoneIsWelcome.org, or call 2-1-1 or 1-800-621-4636.

- Visit a participating bank or credit union and open an account through Bank on Seattle-King County.
  They'll answer your questions and help you open an account that's right for you.

- Bring identification.
  To open a checking account, you'll need to bring your primary ID. You can use a driver's license or other government-issued ID, or the Mexican Matricula card, as primary ID. You may need a second form of ID such as a utility bill or other ID card. Because you can earn interest on savings accounts and some checking accounts, you may also need your Social Security number or an Individual Taxpayer Identification Number.

### Learn to make the most of your money.

Bank on Seattle-King County can help you learn how to use your new account, stay on budget, improve your credit rating, pay off debt, and more.

> Visit www.EveryoneIsWelcome.org, or call 2-1-1 or 1-800-621-4636 to find out about money management classes.

### Banking Q&A

Why should I use a checking account?
It's convenient, safe, and a lot less expensive than using a check cashing service. And you can't lose your money or have it stolen while it's in the account.

What does it cost to cash my paycheck?
NOTHING! It is absolutely free to cash your paycheck at your financial institution. Also, you can arrange for direct deposit of your paycheck or other checks and be able to use your money right away.

Is my money safe?
Yes, your money is safe. Even if something happens to your bank, the federal government will make sure you get your money back.

What else can my bank or credit union do for me?

Money transfers.
Send money to family and friends.

ATM/Debit Cards.
Access your money for free through your bank or credit union's ATM network.

Online bill paying.
Pay your bills online without having to mail a check.

Why spend hundreds of dollars a year at a check cashing company when you can deposit your own checks and pay your bills at no additional cost?

Banking on Opportunity
A Scan of the Evolving Field of Bank On Initiatives
US DEPARTMENT OF THE TREASURY 87
Office of Financial Education and Financial Access

## Appendix 13: Financial Assessment Plan

Bank on Seattle – King County
Assessment of Financial Institutions for
Advertising, Printing and Financial Incentives for Financial Education
May 28, 2008

To participate in Bank on Seattle-King County, every institution would contribute an initial amount:

$1,000 (for institutions with 10 or fewer branches in King County)
$1,500 (for institutions with 11-20 branches in King County)
$2,500 (for institutions with more than 20 branches in King County)

In addition, every institution would contribute a set amount per branch:

- $450 per branch for the first ten branches
- $400 per branch for the 11th through the 20th branches
- $350 per branch for the 21st through the 30th branches
- $300 per branch for the 31st through 40th branches
- $250 per branch for the 41st through 50th branches
- $200 per branch for the 51st through 60th branches
- $150 per branch for the 61st through 70th branches
- $100 per branch for each branch over 70 branches

Example # 1: Financial institution X has 7 branches in Seattle and King County. Its assessment would be $4,150 ($1,000 to participate + $3,150 for seven branches @ $450 per branch)

Example # 2: Financial institution Y has 54 branches in Seattle and King County. Its assessment would be $20,800 ($2,500 to participate + $4,500 for the first 10 branches @ $450 per branch + $4,000 for the next 10 branches @ $400 per branch + $3,500 for the next 10 branches@ $350 per branch +$3,000 for the next 10 branches @ $300 per branch + $2,500 for the next 10 branches@ $250 per branch + $800 for the final four branches @ $200 per branch)

Please Note:
- The financial assessment is based on the total number of branches each institution has in Seattle and King County. Each institution will report the number of their branches that are located within Seattle/King County.
- Funds will be used for printing and placement of marketing materials, advertising, and printing and mailing of outreach materials, and public relations.
- Depending on the number (and size) of financial institutions that ultimately decide to participate, we anticipate that the proposed financial assessment plan will raise from $150,000 to $200,000.
- Our marketing firms estimates that the minimum amount we'll need for advertising/PR is from $150,000 to $200,000.
- This assessment plan is for two years. We would like to have as much of the funds up front as possible because printing and advertising expenses will be greatest at the beginning of the initiative. Some institutions may need to provide half of their assessment soon and then half later on.
- In the second year of the initiative, we may wish to raise additional funds for more advertising and PR, but no participating institution will be obligated to contribute more than their initial assessment.
- Institutions will contribute their funds to a 501 c 3 organization.

## Appendix 14: Financial Education Content Standards

**bank on**
SEATTLE-KING COUNTY
Everyone is welcome

### Financial Education Standards

| Topic | Objective by the end of this module participants will: | To achieve the objective, participants will be able to | Class discussions may include |
|---|---|---|---|
| Financial goal setting | Be able to set financial goals and meet them | • Identify important short and long-term financial goals<br>• Identify steps to reach their goals<br>• Create a written plan to accomplish their goals<br>• Identify benchmarks that help track success with respect to reaching their goals | • Financial hopes and dreams<br>• Talk about personal views on money<br>• Habits and customs when they were growing up<br>• How their current family relates to money<br>• Managing money in the household<br>• Changes they would like to make to better use their money<br>• The difference between short- and long-term goals |
| Controlling your money | Understand how to manage their money successfully | • Specify savings goals they have<br>• Identify relevant income and expense categories they deal with<br>• Manage cash flow to pay bills on time<br>• Create a savings and spending plan to estimate monthly income and expenses<br>• Identify strategies they can employ to decrease spending and increase income<br>• Track their periodic expenses<br>• Adjust their savings and spending plans as life-situation changes | • Managing their money because "every dollar has a job to do"<br>• Sharing ideas about how to develop the habit of writing down all income and expenses<br>• How controlling their money better can help you increase savings to meet their goals<br>• The importance of planning their expenses and checking their plan against reality<br>• The importance of "paying yourself first"<br>• Living within their means<br>• Strategies to pay down debt quickly<br>• Why reducing debt is a form of saving |
| Checking accounts | Understand how to use a checking account responsibly | • State the benefits of using a checking account<br>• Determine which checking account works best for them<br>• Identify the steps involved in opening a checking account<br>• Deposit and withdraw money from a checking account<br>• Write checks correctly to pay bills<br>• Reconcile their checking account by using a check register<br>• Avoid overdrafts and other necessary fees<br>• How to bank online | • Ways they can assure that their money is safe<br>• Why using a checking account makes sense for them<br>• Accessing money through debit cards, checks or ATMs<br>• Automatically depositing pay checks and benefit checks<br>• The amount they save by using a checking account vs. using check cashers<br>• Purchasing what they need using online banking<br>• Strategies to avoid overdraft fees<br>• Strategies to ensure they pay bills on time<br>• Availability of Bank on Seattle-King County accounts<br>• Experiences they have had with a bank or credit union in the past<br>• General differences between credit unions and banks |

| Topic | Objective by the end of this module participants will: | To achieve the objective, participants will be able to | Class discussions may include |
|---|---|---|---|
| Savings | Understand the importance of saving money to improve their life situation | • Explain the importance of saving<br>• How to get started with savings<br>• Identify different ways to save including regular savings accounts, CDs, IRAs, savings bonds, and other savings options<br>• Describe the concept of interest<br>• Determine goals towards which they want to save | • Growing their money, the miracle of compound interest<br>• Choose the best savings option to achieve their goal<br>• Paying off debt to help them meet a savings goal<br>• Connections between saving and building credit<br>• Connections between saving and borrowing for major purchases<br>• Connections between saving and building wealth |
| Credit and credit history | Understand how to establish and maintain good credit | • How to get and read their credit report<br>• Build credit, one step at a time<br>• Repair credit<br>• Acquire secured and unsecured loans<br>• Understand factors creditors look for when making credit decisions<br>• Know the costs and benefits of borrowing money<br>• Apply for credit | • Why good credit can work for them<br>• Why using "rent to own", payday loans and refund anticipation loans may not be worth it<br>• The pros and cons of having your credit in both your and your spouse's/partner's name<br>• Credit building steps:<br>  1. Get a credit card. Buy something with it, and then pay it off quickly.<br>  2. Get a small loan from your bank. Pay it back on time |
| Credit Cards | Be able to use credit cards wisely | • How and when to use a credit card<br>• Choose a credit card that meets their needs and has best interest rates<br>• Know what a credit card costs<br>• Identify steps to take when a credit card is lost or stolen<br>• How to read your monthly statement | • Deciding for yourself whether you need a credit card<br>• Typical credit card tricks and scams<br>• The risks of using a credit card too much<br>• Questions to ask about annual fees, interest rates, grace periods, over limit fees |
| Consumer Rights | Know their legal rights and how to protect their finances and identity | • Protect their money<br>• Understand the importance of protecting their identity<br>• Have the ability to advocate for their rights<br>• Understand consumer protection laws, consumer protection agencies, and discrimination in lending | • Rules to protect their money in the bank<br>• Rules to protect them when applying for a loan<br>• Ways to monitor their finances and identity<br>• Online banking risks; phishing, unsecured sites<br>• What to do when their identity is stolen<br>• Preparing for financial disaster |
| Consumer loans | Know how they could use consumer loans responsibly to make a large purchase | • Differentiate between types of consumer loans<br>• Understand the factors lenders use to make loan decisions<br>• Describe the cost of borrowing money<br>• Compare the benefits and disadvantages of different loan offers | • Picking a loan that meets their needs<br>• Difference between installment loans and rent to own services<br>• Things to know when borrowing to buy a car<br>• Advantages and disadvantages of borrowing against a home |

Appendix 14-Financial Education Content standards.doc
10/13/2011

| Topic | Objective<br>by the end of this<br>module participants will: | To achieve the objective, participants will be able to | Class discussions may include |
|---|---|---|---|
| Home ownership | Buy a home when they are ready | • Understand the benefits of renting vs. owning a home<br>• Identify steps required to buy a home<br>• Purchase a recent merge Credit Report (30 days)<br>• Create a homeownership action plan<br>• Complete Washington State Housing Finance Commission homeownership workshop<br>• Participate in at least 1 individual one-on-one homeownership counseling session | • Questions to ask before deciding to buy a home<br>• Keeping their home and building value<br>• Basic terms used in mortgage transactions<br>• Advantages and disadvantages of different mortgage options |
| Personal taxes | Know how to maximize their tax return | • Understand how to complete a W-4 to maximize their withholdings<br>• Understand how to file for the EITC and other tax credits | • Tax filing and tax credits for undocumented workers<br>• Tax credits for children and families<br>• Getting a big tax refund is not necessarily a good thing<br>• Split refunds as an opportunity to save<br>• Alternatives to high cost tax preparation (availability of free tax prep through UWKC and ACORN EITC campaigns) |
| (Optional) Insurance | Be able to describe the benefits of insurance | • Understand the value of rental insurance, driver's insurance, disability insurance, homeowners insurance | • Insurance options / pro and con |

Appendix 14-Financial Education Content standards.doc
10/13/2011

## Appendix 15: Financial Education Brochure

### New Account Tips and Tricks

> Keep track of your money.
Use your check register to write down every time you write a check or use your ATM or debit card.

> Use online banking.
It's easy to use and keep track of your transactions. You can check how much money you have in your account whenever you want.

> Balance your account.
Carefully read your statements and compare them to your check register. This will help you catch errors.

> Spend only what you have.
Writing a check or making an ATM or debit card withdrawal or purchase for more money than you have in your checking account can cost you a lot in fees.

> Keep your PIN secret.
The personal identification number (PIN) that you use with your debit card should be kept secret. If someone else finds out what your PIN is, they can steal your money.

> Keep your checks to yourself.
Don't sign blank checks or let anyone else use them.

> Use direct deposit.
Your paycheck will go straight into your account on payday. No more waiting in lines, and you can use your money right away.

> Avoid ATM fees.
Only use ATMs provided by your bank or credit union.

To learn more about managing your money, contact one of these organizations.

**American Financial Solutions**
www.myfinancialgoals.org
888 282-5811

**Consumer Counseling Northwest**
www.ccnw.org
253 589-1858 ext 307

**El Centro de la Raza**
www.elcentrodelaraza.org
206 957-4646

**Hopelink**
www.hope-link.org
425 869-6000

**International District Housing Alliance**
www.apialliance.org
206 623-5132

**Multi-Service Center**
www.multi-servicecenter.com
253 954-4406

**Neighborhood House**
www.nhwa.com
206 461-4554 ext 30

**Parkview Services**
www.parkviewservices.org
206 529-4114

**United Indians of All Tribes**
www.unitedindians.org
206 285-4425

**Urban League of Metropolitan Seattle**
www.urbanleague.org
206 461-3792 ext 3004

**YWCA**
wwwywcaworks.org
206 336-4601

**bank on**
SEATTLE–KING COUNTY
Everyone is welcome

### CREATING YOUR FINANCIAL FUTURE
Making the most of your new bank account

For more information about Bank on Seattle-King County, visit www.EveryoneisWelcome.org or call 211.

### Banking Q&A

**Why should I use a checking account?**
It's convenient. You can't lose your money or have it stolen while it's in the account. You can write checks to pay your bills. You can sign up for online banking and have your bills paid from your checking account automatically. You can use a debit card to get cash whenever you need to.

**What does it cost to cash my paycheck?**
NOTHING! It is absolutely free to cash your paycheck at your financial institution. However, if you do not have direct deposit, you may have to wait a few days to access your money if you do not already have enough money in the account to cover the check. Talk to your bank or credit union and employer about starting direct deposit.

**What is a savings account?**
Savings accounts usually pay higher interest than checking accounts. You can deposit money in or withdraw money from your savings account, but you can't write checks with it.

**How can I avoid bouncing checks?**
Know how much you have in your account!
A substantial fee is charged when you write a check or make a withdrawal from an ATM or use your ATM or debit card to make a purchase for more money than you have in your account. A fee may be charged every time you try to take out more than is in your account. Be sure you have enough money in your account to cover your checks, withdrawals, and purchases. Some banks and credit unions have features that help you avoid paying fees, for example, by declining your purchase or withdrawal request if you don't have enough money in your account. For more specific bank and credit union information, go to www.EveryoneisWelcome.org and click on "Avoid Overdraft Fees" under "How Do I Open an Account."

**Is my money safe?**
Yes, your money is safe. Even if something happens to your bank, the federal government will make sure you get your money back (up to $250,000).

**What does it cost to have a checking account?**
Most Bank on Seattle-King County banks and credit unions offer checking accounts that don't cost anything. A few charge a low monthly fee.

**How do I know how much money I have in my checking account?**
You will get a check register when you open your account. Use it any time you:
- Write a check.
- Make a purchase or withdrawal with your ATM or debit card.
- Deposit money in your account.
- Have money automatically deposited in or withdrawn from your account.

**What else can my bank or credit union do for me?**

*Money Transfers.*
Send money to family and friends.

*Online Bill Paying.*
Pay your bills online without having to mail a check.

*ATM/Debit Cards.*
Access your money for free through your bank or credit union's ATM network.

**bank on**
SEATTLE–KING COUNTY
Everyone is welcome

Appendix 16: Template for Clear, Written Explanation of Fees

## ** SAMPLE**
### (To be customized by each institution)
### Bank on Seattle-King County
### Explanation of Fees, Rates, and Procedures*

There is no initial cost to you to open an account. However, you need to put a minimum of $__ into the account to open it.

No minimum monthly balance is required. You can let the balance go to zero at any time. However, if you do not use the account for 6 months, it may be closed.

You will not be charged fees to write checks, deposit money, or take out money (if you use our ATM machines). You can do any of those activities as often as you like at no cost.

You will not be charged for depositing a check. However, you may not be able to receive cash back from the check for __ days, unless you have an equivalent amount available in your account. If a hold is placed on your deposit items, you will be informed at the time of the deposit or within 24 business hours. You may have your employer deposit your paycheck directly into your account. It is free and it will allow you to receive cash from the check immediately.

If you write a check for more money than you have in the account, you will be charged $ ___. You may also get charged $__ per day. [Other NSF/OD consequences] The first time you do this, you should call us as soon as possible and let us know that you are a Bank on Seattle-King County customer and should not be charged this fee the first time. [Other procedures for NSF/OD] After the first time, we will _____.

You will not be charged a fee to use our network of ATMs. However, if you use an ATM outside of our network, then you may be charged $__ by us and an additional amount by the ATM network that you use.

You may also open a savings account. You need $__ for your initial deposit. It will cost _____. [Fees/costs associated with a savings account]

[Benefits/incentives for opening a savings account]

You may do your banking online for [free/$__]. To do this, go to [website].

A money order or cashier's check costs $___.

[Cost/fees associated with equity lines/small dollar loans, if available]

If you wish to send money overseas, it will cost $___.

*This is not a complete list of contractual obligations and should be used only in conjunction with _____ as required by regulators. Services and Fees Brochures are subject to change.

Effective: [Date]

www.ingramcontent.com/pod-product-compliance
Lightning Source LLC
Chambersburg PA
CBHW080315290526
45790CB00005B/2050